P9-DHH-850

Text **Claude Lebédel** Photographs **Catherine Bibollet**
Translation **Dédicace**

UNDERSTANDING THE TRAGEDY OF THE CATHARS

Editions OUEST-FRANCE

Contents

6 Problems of vocabulary, diverging viewpoints

12 The context and the players

34 The Cathar religion

46 The unfolding of events

112 In the footsteps of the Cathars…

122 Appendix

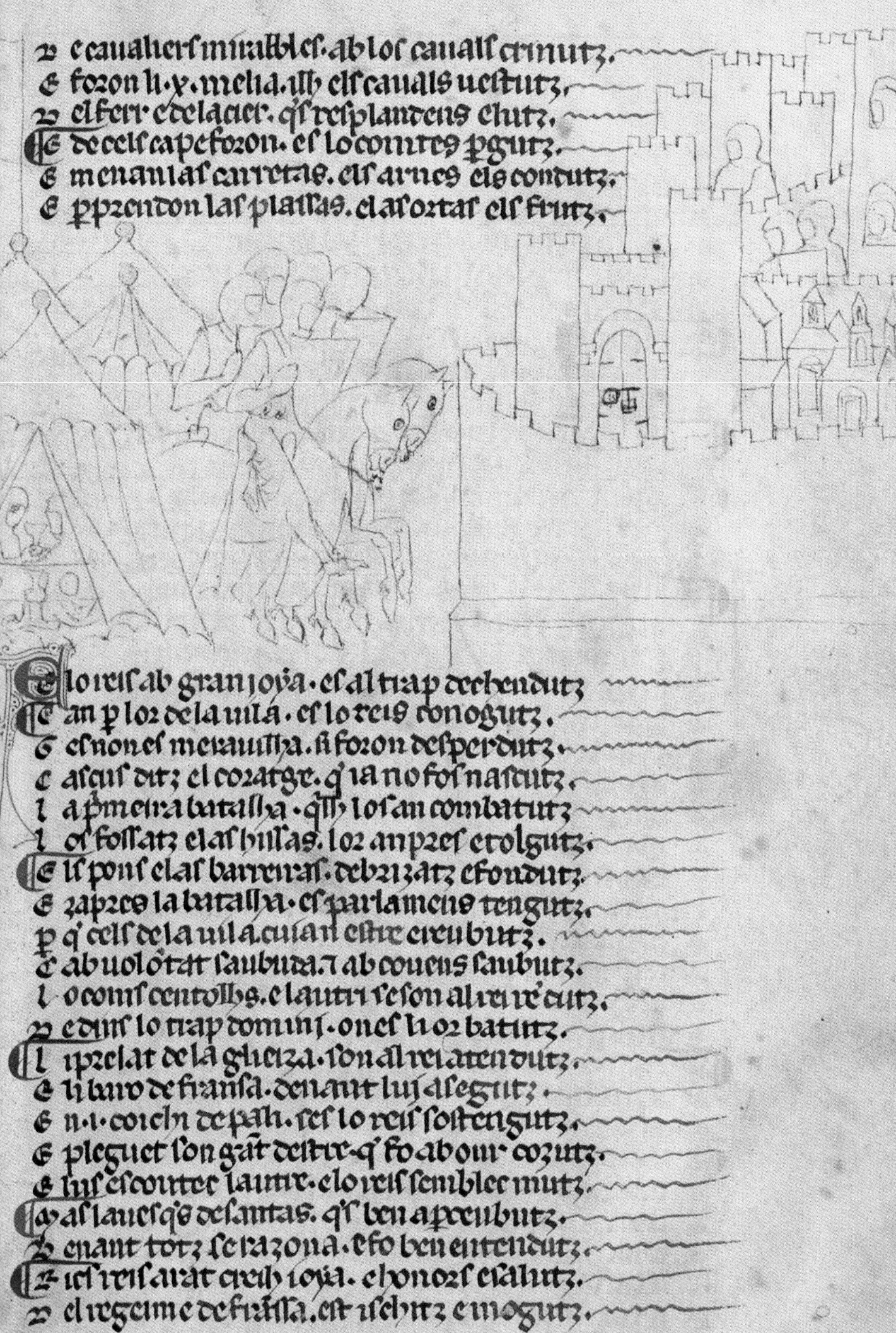

.le seti de marmanda caut le filh del rey de fransa la pres.

De caualiers mirables. ab los caualls crinutz.
E foron li .x. melia. ilh els cauals uestutz.
Del ferr e de l'acier. q's resplandens e lutz.
E de cels cap e foron. es lo comtes pergutz.
E menauas carretas. els arnes els condutz.
E prendon las plassas. e las ortas els frutz.

E lo reis ab gran ioya. es al trap deschendutz
Can per lor de la uila. es lo reis conogutz.
E es non es merauilha. si foron desperdutz.
C ascus ditz el coratge. q' ia no fos nascutz.
L a primeira batalha. q'ilh los an combatutz
L os fossatz e las lissas. lor an pres e tolgutz.
E ls pons e las barreiras. debrizatz e fondutz.
E zapres la batalha. es parlamens tengutz.
P er q' cels de la uila. cuian estre receubutz.
E ab uolontat saubuda. e ab couens saubutz.
L o coms centolhs. e lautri reson al rei rendutz.
D edins lo trap domini. on es li orz batutz.
E li prelat de la gleiza. son al rei atendutz.
E li baro de fransa. denant luy asegutz.
E n .i. coissin de pali. ses lo reis sostengutz.
E pleguet son gant destre. q' fo ab our cozutz.
E lus escoutet lautre. e lo reis semblet mutz.
M as l'auesq's de santas. q's ben apercebutz.
D enant totz se razona. e fo ben entendutz.
S enher reis arat creih ioya. e honors e salutz.
D el regisme de fransa. est iselitz e mogutz.

Problems of vocabulary, diverging viewpoints

Much has been written about the Cathars, much and even too much in the sense that ideas often very removed from reality have been put forward about them. Differences in interpretation have meant that the tragic events which occupied a major place in the history of our country have been given an almost supernatural dimension. In order to understand all the facts on what happened over a period of almost two centuries (the very last Cathar Perfect was eliminated in 1321), it is best to start with simple ideas which, gradually, will become clearer as the description and analysis of this human tragedy, in which intolerance imposed its absolute law, is revealed. In that way, the reader interested in following a route around the Cathar Castles will be able to set out with a certain amount of information and ideas which he will be able to complete and diversify with the wealth of historical, pseudo-historical, and even fantastical literature on the subject of the Cathars and Catharism.

The first point which needs to be clarified concerns the vocabulary. It is important to note that neither the "Cathars", the Christian priests or monks, nor the Inquisition used this term. The most common expression was the "Albigensian heretics" and that within this category, the Inquisitors singled out the "Perfects", namely the priests, or heretical preachers. The term "Albigensian" may be explained by the fact that Catharism flourished in the region of Albi.

Several terms may be used to refer to the opposing side, namely those whose aim was to eliminate the Cathar heresy: the crusaders, the papacy, the French. In the latter case, the reference complies with history since at that time the word "French" referred to the inhabitants of Ile-de-France, the centre of the slowly emerging French kingdom. It was from this region that the majority of the opposition originated, consisting of members of the army (and especially their leader Simon de Montfort) which resolved the Cathar problem through the use of force (and, as we will see, under often horrific conditions!).

< ***Chanson de la Croisade des Albigeois* written by William of Tudela at the start of the 13th century.** Written in a Cathar cultural context, it offers an insight into what the general atmosphere might have been at that time.

Bibliothèque nationale de France, Paris, Ms fr. 25425, f° 231.

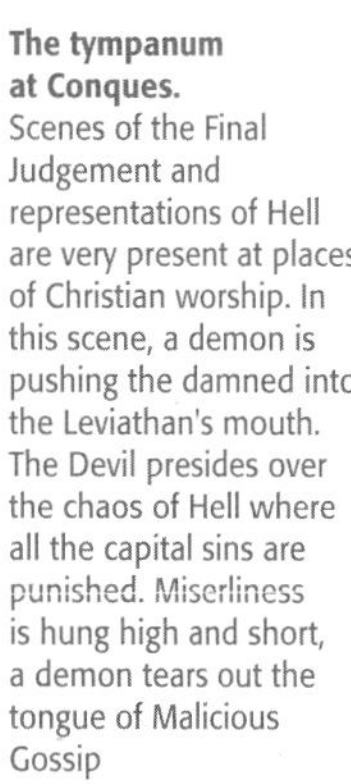

The tympanum at Conques.
Scenes of the Final Judgement and representations of Hell are very present at places of Christian worship. In this scene, a demon is pushing the damned into the Leviathan's mouth. The Devil presides over the chaos of Hell where all the capital sins are punished. Miserliness is hung high and short, a demon tears out the tongue of Malicious Gossip
Photo J. Debru.

The word "Cathar"

This word is used to refer to two categories of people: these may be followers of the religion of the same name, or priests of this religion, otherwise known as "Perfects". But, it should be noted that these people never used the term "Cathar" when referring to their religion, or the term "Perfect". "Cathar" priests were referred to and referred to themselves as "Good Christians" or "Good Men" (as well as "Good Women" because women did not play a minor role in Cathar religion, quite the contrary).

The Inquisition never used the term Cathar to refer to these "heretics". So where did this word come from? It first appeared in 1163, in a sermon by a German monk, Eckbert of Schonau, in reference to heretics he had "fought" against (it is they who in common language we call "Cathars").

Why did the word have such a success when the interested parties and the Inquisition never used it in reference to them? In fact, up until the middle of last century, a different word with regional connotations was used, namely "Albigensians" (which explains the expression the "Albigensian crusade"). It was Charles Schmidt who is said to have employed the expression "Albigensian Cathars" in 1849.

It remains for us to find the initial meaning of the word "Cathar". Common opinion makes reference to Greek with the word "Purs" (it is easy to see how this may have, mistakenly, given rise to the word "Perfect"). This etymology does not have any foundation, but there is another theory acknowledged by some specialists but refuted by others. This time it is German which provides the explanation. In the Middle Ages, in the Rhine region, the cat was believed to be an incarnation of the Devil. In Middle High German, "cat" was pronounced "Katte" and the word "heretic" or "Katzer" in German comes from "Ketter". All are based on the same roots. Therefore, in the Middle Ages, Cathars (heretics) were referred to as those who kissed a cat's backside to honour Satan.

Whatever its origins, the word "Cathar" has become common usage and will be used throughout this book.

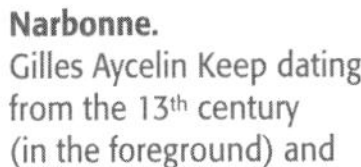

Narbonne.
Gilles Aycelin Keep dating from the 13th century (in the foreground) and the Archbishops' Palace.

Perfect

This word comes from the Inquisition and was never used by the Cathars. It comes from the Latin term hereticus perfectus which means "accomplished, complete heretic" and does not have the positive connotation that the word "perfect" has nowadays. In the eyes of the Inquisitors, this was the most accomplished form of heretic, meaning the priests or preachers (to use a term which those concerned never used), those who spread the Cathar word and who, as a result, were hounded and hunted down.

The Cathar religion tolerated equality between men and women when it came to preaching and carrying out rites.

Carcassonne.
Restoration work, sometimes abusive, dating from the 19th century offers today's visitors an insight into what this town might have looked like during the crusades.

Feudal society: the King, the clergy and the aristocracy in western medieval society.
15th century manuscript, extract from *De informatione principum* by Gilles de Rome, illumination by Maître de Talbot. Bibliothèque Nationale, Paris, Ms fr. 126, f° 7.

The way in which, over the centuries, the Cathar affair has been understood is the second point that needs to be clarified. Every period has made its contribution to the diverging viewpoints. From the 14th to the 18th century, this episode was shrouded in a black cloud, either as a result of guilt or, more likely, because the power of religious practice and the role of Christian, Catholic religion was such that everything that happened during the Albigensian crusades was seen, in some respects, as being "normal".

Then, with the advent of tolerance, came the evocation of the martyrs of the freedom of conscience. Without wishing to make too many easy comparisons, it should be noted that the revolt of the Calvinist partisans was situated in a region not very far from the region of Albi.

An opposing opinion emerged with the Republican School of the 19th century and, in the first half of the 20th century, the Cathars were seen as subversives of national unity owing to the regional dimension of their movement (Occitan language, etc.).

However, since the return in force of regionalist ideas, there has been a tendency to move towards the opposite extreme whereby Occitanism is confused with Catharism with the first being seen as the latter and vice versa. Did the Cathars really know that they were defending a culture, a civilisation opposed to that of the French from the North? The documents available do not support this rather simplistic theory.

But, this leads to a third question: was the Cathar affair a question of religion or politics? In actual fact it was both religious and political because, as we will see, the overlap between religious and political factors was a necessary consequence of the nature of medieval civilisation in the 12th and 13th centuries. Although solving the Cathar problem led to the complete absorption of the entire Occitan geographic area by the Kingdom of France, it cannot be said that this objective was foremost in the minds of those who intervened from the outside; the quarrels between the King of France and the papacy on this subject were significant. But, it is true that the Kings of France did take advantage of the situation during the final phases of the crusade.

To conclude these few general preliminary remarks, it is necessary for us to quickly recall some divergences in interpretation in order not to have to return to them later.

The first, relatively innocent but entirely false, concerns the Holy Grail. In 1183, Chrétien de Troyes started writing Perceval on request from Philip of Alsace, the Count of Flanders, who clearly sided with the Church against the Cathars. The themes developed in this work are the complete opposite of Cathar theories because, among other things, reference is made to the Trinity, the Redeeming Passion, Marriage, the Incarnation, etc. Despite this, some people have wanted to see the Albigensian crusade as an operation designed to rob the Cathars of their treasure, namely the Holy Grail (meaning, according to legend, the dish used for Christ's Last Supper and the vase containing the blood spilt by Christ when on the cross).

Which texts from the period tell us about the history of the Cathars?

The most important text (which should be read with great caution because it greatly favours the crusade) is the Historia Albigensis by Peter of Vaux de Cernay. As a companion and friend of Simon de Montfort, the author provides great detail about the latter's behaviour and the reactions of the crusaders.

William of Puylaurens was the chaplain of the Count of Toulouse, Raymond VII. He left a Chronicle in which information may be found about both sides.

The *Chanson de la Croisade des Albigeois* is the work of William of Tudela (in Navarre). This text actually comprises two separate parts: one written directly by William, who probably travelled from Navarre to Montauban in 1199 and encountered many participants or witnesses of the Cathar affair. The second part is much more poetic than the first and the author is not known but he is probably from Toulouse.

These three texts help us to understand the general atmosphere and the unfolding of events, but do not expect to find a historic presentation in the modern-day scientific sense of the word.

Just as fanciful is the fantastical comparison made by some between Cathar religion and certain aspects of Hinduism (some even go so far as to make a direct link). It is necessary to be very moderate and careful on this subject. The taste for exoticism and indefinable distant shores does not concur with the thoughtful and methodical analysis of what we know about the Cathars and nothing permits such a simplistic comparison.

The same applies, but in a much more dangerous manner, to the efforts made by some to reduce Cathar religion to the practice of sun worship and even to rites such as those taught by some sects.

Let us return to the facts. In the second half of the 12th century, in an area demarcated by the towns of Toulouse, Albi, Carcassonne and Foix, a religious movement developed which the Catholic hierarchy and the papacy considered to be heretical. This movement followed in the footsteps of other similar ones, but this time, in the eyes of the established religious order, the phenomenon was seen as being particularly dangerous because it questioned the temporal power of the Church and developed outside the fundamental framework of the feudal system. Everything ended fifty years later in a bloodbath with the integration of the region into the kingdom of France.

This rather short and apparently simplistic summary hides a number of questions for which it is not possible to provide answers for the entire period and for all the events which took place. What was the true basis of Cathar ideas and, in particular, what role did the rural nobility play? Did the Count of Toulouse want to play a political role or did he always find himself carried along by events? At what point did the King of France decide to take political advantage of the situation? Did the papacy simply want to eradicate heresy or did it also want to assert its theocratic conception of the world?

Finally, it should be added that the word "heresy" in this text does not in any way imply a value judgement about the deviant or non-deviant nature of Cathar doctrine in relation to Christian doctrine. It is used out of simple convenience, in the same way as the term Cathar.

The context and the players

Whenever the word "Cathar" is pronounced, the name of Montségur Castle immediately comes to mind, but the taking of this, the last (or nearly the last) bastion of Cathar religion, was only the final episode in a process which started much earlier.

The feudal regime

It is not possible to understand the unfolding of the events that led to the Cathar tragedy unless one understands the main mechanisms of the fundamental feature of society in the 12th and 13th centuries, namely the feudal regime.

What did this involve? It was the framework within which the relationships between the different layers of society were organised and, more precisely, the rules governing the relationships between the lords. The Cathar crisis broke out at a time when this social system was at its zenith, its "classic" period.

The feudal system corresponds to a series of institutions defining the obligations of service and obedience of "vassals" towards "lords" and of protection and upkeep of "suzerains" towards "vassals".

Aerial view of Montségur.
This castle was one of the many stages in the fight against the Cathars.
Photo R. Cast.

The fortified city of Carcassonne.
The ramparts and the castle seen from the covered way.

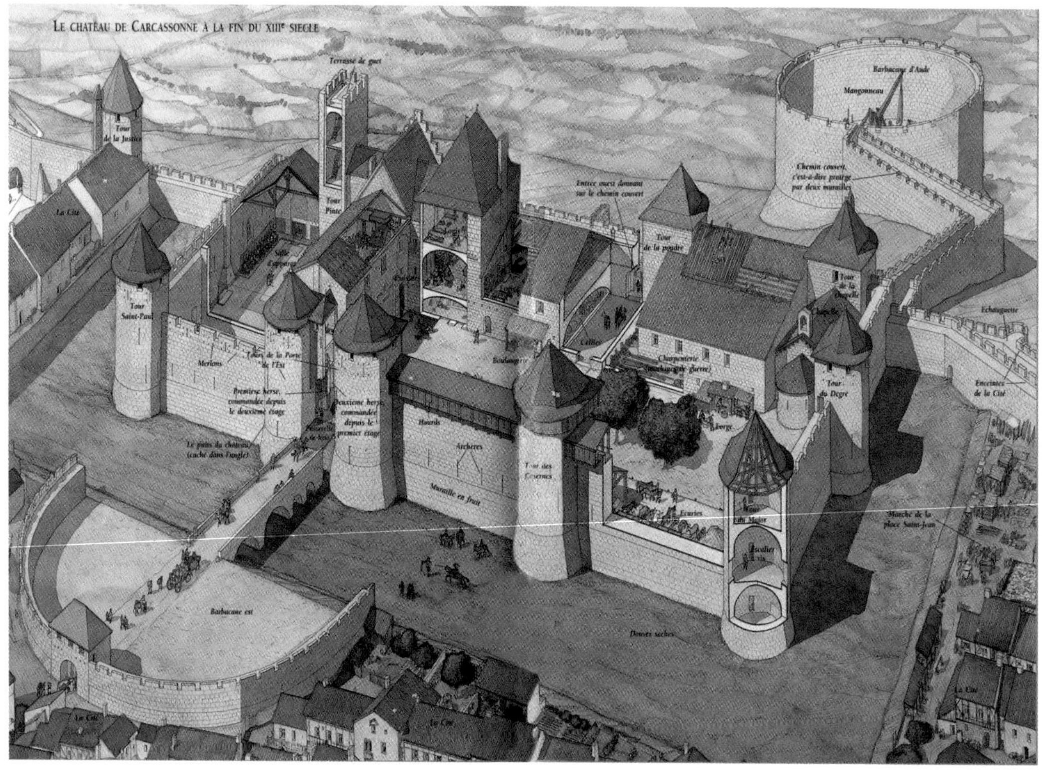

Carcassonne castle at the end of the 13th century.
Reproduction drawing by Jean-Claude Golvin, © Géo.

The feudal castle

In about 1,000 AD, feudal castles started to be built in stone. Previously the general layout was a mound with an earth and wood levee. The mound of earth was surrounded by a ditch and surmounted by a tower or keep which served as a residence or as a surveillance post, usually rectangular in shape. Around the keep, lay a courtyard with a fence and a ditch.

A stone-built structure greatly helped to improve protection. The keep became a huge square structure. At the time of the Albigensian crusade, the shape of castles changed in order to take account of the new machines of war (catapults): more towers in addition to keeps, alteration to the angle of loopholes, switch from rectangle-shaped buildings to circular-shaped buildings, doubling of the protecting walls, construction of taluses to reduce sapping work, etc.

Consequently, military assaults by crusaders on Cathar castles involved long and costly operations because complex machines were sometimes used requiring qualified personnel, large amounts of money and a plan.

Traditionally, an assault on a castle was gradual involving the use of covered galleries ("chattes") or rolling towers, and even the excavation of tunnels (and remember that explosives did not yet exist).

A battering ram beneath a rolling frame known as a "chatte".
Photo R. Beffeyte.

Lords' rights

The seigniory and the parish were the two basic units of daily life in the Middle Ages. There may have been a geographic correspondence between them, but a seigniory could also (frequently) cover several parishes and, more rarely, a parish could belong to two seigniories. In order to understand what it represented for a lord to lose his rights (something relatively common as a result of the unforeseen events of the crusade against the Albigensians), it is necessary to understand what these rights involved.

The lord's rights involved two aspects: land (over property) and banal (over people).

The land of the lord's domain comprised the reserve, which the lord managed directly, and tenures, farms which the lord conceded to farmers (tenants). In return the farmers owed services to the lord which took the form of corvée (labour, harvests), namely forced labour on the reserve.

The so-called banal right corresponded to the power to collect a tax or taille, to judge, to punish and to decree (for example when cereal or grape harvests could commence).

Of course, the interlinking network of vassalic ties within the feudal system complicated matters; in actual fact, it was possible for a tenure to depend on one lord for farming and on several lords for banal rights (for example, one lord for justice, another for taille and a third for the use of a mill).

After the fall of the Roman Empire and with the "Barbarian" invasions (meaning that the people did not speak Latin), a very unstable and often anarchic system was established in what would later become France. The structure that nowadays we call the State had practically disappeared and, in particular, security was no longer guaranteed. Quite naturally, a clientele-based system, with what we would now refer to as private militia, developed. An increasing number of free men (meaning neither slaves nor serfs) came under the protection of other, more powerful, free men. In order to ensure upkeep, that is the subsistence of the person who had obtained the protection of a powerful figure, the suzerain was required to provide him with a piece of land under relatively precarious conditions, namely for the duration of his dependence on this person.

These two elements became so closely interlinked that, by the time of Charlemagne, they had become inseparable: vassality (the state of dependence on a powerful figure) and profit (the granting of a piece of land to ensure the vassal's upkeep and the means required to enable him to provide assistance to a powerful figure) had merged.

At the time of the Cathars, the system was general practice in France. It was exported to England by the Norman Conquest and to the Near East by the crusaders. Almost all free men with a military background, able to fight on horseback, and with land, followed the principles of vassality, with the duties and obligations which will be explained later. This meant that solving the Cathar problem had to take into account and, more precisely, use, the mechanisms of the feudal system.

This system may be compared to a pyramid with dependency links between its different levels: at the bottom, the small vassals with nobody beneath them, followed by a suzerain, who was in the same position of vassality but with a more powerful lord. But the pyramid can be very complex, with one suzerain being the vassal of another suzerain, etc., and maybe even involving interlinking situations.

Homage to the suzerain. Very precise codes governed the relationships between the different members of feudal society. The suzerain and the vassal were joined by a contract of vassality which involved clear procedures.
Copy of a manuscript from 1373-1376. Bibliothèque Nationale, Paris, Ms fr. 20082, f° 171.

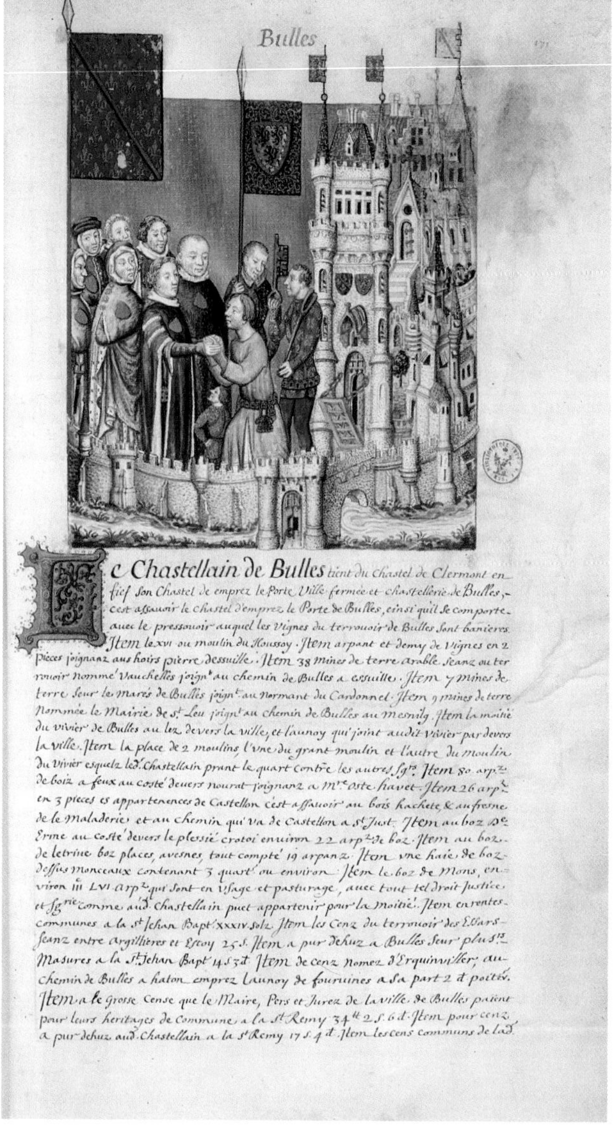

Therefore, the basis of the contract between the suzerain and the vassal involved land which the first entrusted to the second under usufruct, giving use of the land to the second, although he did not own it. The suzerain also granted the vassal his protection in return for assistance in war, at court, and in exchange for various dues.

People in the Middle Ages did not have a taste for abstraction which was why a contract was sealed by a ceremony. In the case of the vassality contract, this involved the vassal paying homage to the suzerain by kneeling before him, placing his hands in those of the lord, giving his oath of fealty and receiving a kiss from the suzerain.

During the Cathar tragedy, the mechanisms of the feudal system were fully operational: the lords asked their vassals for military assistance in order to accompany them on the crusade against the Albigensian-Cathars. Gradually, this notion of military assistance was more clearly defined and covered a limited period: ost (for example 40 days of consecutive service, after which the suzerain had to pay a sum of money), or be carried out in a specific region. It could also be replaced by payment in kind (horses or weapons) or in cash.

Naturally, land, the basis of the contract, had stopped being a usufruct and had become hereditary, but the practice of the homage and the oath continued. The Church too became part of the feudal system, with a lord being the suzerain for land granted to a chapel in return for which a cleric paid homage to him. Conversely, a bishop might have found himself with an estate within his fief for which a secular lord paid homage to him.

In feudal law, the suzerain had the right to depose a vassal if he did not respect his oath and put his fief in danger. Generalising this practice, the papacy attempted to depose lords who protected heretics, replacing them with other lords who followed the papacy's instructions. In this way, the papacy succeeded in rising above normal suzerains.

Condemnation and torture of the Amalricians (supporters of Amaury de Chartres) in the presence of Philip Augustus.
This picture does not concern the Cathar tragedy but it does offer an idea of the way in which the ceremony proceeded.
Illumination by Jean Fouquet, extract from *Les Grandes Chroniques de France*. 15th century manuscript. Bibliothèque Nationale, Paris. Ms fr. 6465 f° 236.

The notion of heresy and its development

There have always been heretics, namely people considered as such in the eyes of a religion which believed that any deviation from its fundamental principles risked endangering its unity. But, until the 11th century, heretics within the Christian religion did not involve large groups of people, only a few individuals. Things changed greatly after 1,000 AD. In 1022, for the very first time, the King of France ordered death by burning without any legal basis. This execution in Orléans was exceptional. In general, the legal sentence was excommunication accompanied by fasting and the obligation of pilgrimage. Heresy was a purely spiritual affair.

Faced with the inability of this measure alone to suppress heresy as important as that of the Cathars in the 12th century, the Council of Toulouse demanded in 1112 that the temporal power provide a solution and, in 1139, the Second Council of the Lateran recalled that secular power had a duty to persecute heretics. Cooperation was needed between spiritual and temporal power. It was the Fourth Council of the Lateran in 1215 that marked a decisive step in repression, so much so that Innocent III was accused, in some respects, of having created a "society of persecution". Heresy became an offence which secular power had to punish as such whenever spiritual power informed it of the facts. The idea was to reduce everything to unity because diversity was compared to evil and deviance was a serious crime. Heresy was seen as something which disturbed the public order.

Very quickly the situation became favourable to repression. Pope Innocent III associated heresy with the crime of lese-majesty, which led to an automatic death sentence, with the guilty person, owing to his heretical beliefs, having breached the image of compliance with the divine laws which were supposed to reign.

This legal and ideological basis led to the development of the Inquisition and the implementation of its courts throughout Languedoc.

What the Church decreed against the Cathars
(Third Council of the Lateran, 1179)

"Since in Gascony and the regions of Albi and Toulouse and in other places the loathsome heresy has grown so strong that they no longer practise their wickedness in secret, as others do, but proclaim their error publicly and draw the simple and weak to join them, we declare that they and their defenders and those who receive them are under anathema, and we forbid under pain of anathema that anyone should keep or support them in their houses or lands or should trade with them... we decree that they should not be received into the communion of the church and are free from all obligations of loyalty, homage or any obedience.... On these and on all the faithful we enjoin, for the remission of sins, that they oppose this scourge with all their might and by arms protect the Christian people against them. Their goods are to be confiscated and princes free to subject them to slavery... We too trusting in the mercy of God and the authority of the blessed apostles Peter and Paul, grant to faithful Christians who take up arms against them, and who on the advice of bishops or other prelates seek to drive them out, a remission for two years of penance imposed on them."
Later texts simply repeated these measures.
Introduction and translation taken from Decrees of the Ecumenical Councils, ed. Norman P. Tanner.
Extract from Zoé Oldenburg, *Le Bûcher de Montségur*, Gallimard, 1959, p. 389.

The Cistercian abbey of Fontfroide in Aude (south of Narbonne) which has kept its 12th century church, played an important role in the fight against the Cathars. Its Abbot Fulk (no doubt a troubadour turned monk) became the Bishop of Toulouse and was a fierce adversary of the Cathars whom he hounded ruthlessly. It was from this abbey that Pierre de Castelnau set out as the Pope's legate in 1205.

The Church

We must ask the reader again to try to understand the mentality of men (or women) living at the start of the 13th century. For this person, the feudal structure of society was an indisputable principle which governed all aspects of daily life. It was the lord who owned the mill, who demanded a toll for crossing a bridge, who presided over the court, who occupied a prime position in the parish church.

The Church and religion occupied an equally important place in his daily life and its rhythm was dictated by religious celebrations. Apart from purely religious announcements made by priests during sermons, it was also priests who ensured contact with the outside world, who presented the major decisions taken by the bishop or the lord, whether from near or far, as well as any general news which had reached his ears. Also it is important to remember that the civil registry was managed by priests.

The Cistercian abbey of Fontfroide.

It was this entire environment which was put into question by the Cathar heresy. But, what about the different elements of this environment, for example the papacy, the crusades, the religious orders, the means which the Church had at its disposal to fight the heretics, whose numbers had continued to grow over the previous two centuries?

The papacy

The main player in the Cathar affair was the papacy. This can be explained by the fact that the heart of the problem was essentially a religious one, but, today, we have difficulty in understanding the influence of the papacy over politics at that time.

At the decisive moment, namely, when Pope Innocent III decided to launch a crusade against the Cathar heresy, this influence was reinforced by two elements. On the one hand, the papacy had acquired a doctrine justifying in its eyes any possible interventions in the internal affairs of States and, on the other hand, Rome, at that time, was in an exceptionally favourable political situation.

This doctrine was theocracy used by the papacy to assume sovereign authority over all temporal affairs. It was a political doctrine which called upon the postulancy of a need to create a form of government in accordance with a vision of the world believed to be ideal. According to this theory, the papacy was only allowed to exercise political authority directly provided that the person who assumed the role was granted such power by the papacy and was controlled by it. Of course, theocracy was not something which was introduced in one fell swoop, but took several centuries to develop and gain credence. The 13th century was its zenith owing to the outstanding intellectual personality of Innocent III and also because of the gravity of the political and religious events with which the papacy was faced, obliging it to act forcefully and accordingly.

The cloister of the Cistercian abbey of Fontfroide.

Pope Innocent III.
Innocent III was the most representative Pope (1198-1216) of the theocratic theory of pontifical power and was the one who launched the crusade against the Cathars.
Fresco from 1210 in the Monastery of Saint Benedict in Subiaco. AKG-Images.

Innocent III

This Pope played a decisive role in the Cathar affair because it was he who launched the "crusade against the Albigensians". Lothair of Segni was born in Anagni (Italy) in 1160 or 1161 to a noble family. He studied in Rome, in Paris (theology) and in Bologna (canon law). Canon of Saint Peter's Church in Rome (in around 1185), Pope Clement III (1187-1191), who was his maternal uncle, appointed him cardinal in 1190 (at the age of 30). He was elected Pope in 1198 and ruled the Holy See until 1216 in a very active and intelligent manner, never failing to intervene in temporal affairs as a determined and intransigent representative of the theocratic theories which he embodied.

The notion of crusade

The first crusade preached in 1095 in Clermont by Pope Urban II had three clear objectives which were also the same as those for later crusades: to free Jerusalem in order to enable pilgrims to visit the Holy City, to deliver the Christians of Orient from Muslim domination and to drive out the Turks who had laid siege to Constantinople.

The crusaders wore an embroidered cross on their right shoulder (the reason for the term crusade). Their journey and the time spent in the Holy Land was seen as a pilgrimage and the participants benefited from the Church's full indulgence and protection over their property with a moratorium for the payment of debts. All these elements applied to later crusades.

The Albigensian crusade (the one against the Cathars) was different, involving a war against populations which were not "infidels" and attacking heresy at its base, meaning local lay or religious frameworks, by deposing them and replacing them with Catholics loyal to the papacy (which placed the crusade in contradiction with feudal law by using a procedure of expropriation-usurpation).

In 1095, Pope Urban II travelled to Clermont to preach the crusade in the Holy Land.

Manuscript from 1337.
Extract from *Roman de Godefroi* by William of Tyre, illumination by Maître de Fauvel.
Bibliothèque Nationale, Paris. Ms fr. 22495, f° 15.

Fontcaude abbey, 12th century.

At the start of the 13th century, political conditions at the Holy See were very favourable, making it easier for it to place pressure on States to solve the Cathar problem through the use of force. Why? Because Pope Innocent III knew how to make the most of circumstances in order to take advantage of his situation as arbitrator. In 1197, the German Emperor, Henry VI, died leaving a very young son Frederick (born in 1196) whose mother was the last heir to the Kingdom founded by the Normans in Sicily. Two candidates presented themselves as the Emperor's successor. His brother Philip of Swabia and Otto of Brunswick, who both asked the Pope for his support. However, the Pope decided to lend his support to the young Frederick, whom he crowned and treated as his own personal protégé (the situation later evolved greatly but these changes date to after the start of the crusade against the Cathars).

In England, the papacy also succeeded in imposing its ideas following a dispute over the appointment of the Archbishop of Canterbury. In some respects, John Lackland, King of England, was deposed by the Pope (1213), and the King of France, Philip Augustus was invited to seize the Kingdom of England. John Lackland capitulated in order to maintain the throne and submitted to becoming a vassal of the Pope. Thus, the Pope had highlighted and threatened to apply a new rule of feudal law, namely one that made it possible to replace an unworthy suzerain with another whose behaviour was considered by Rome to be more appropriate.

In this manner, the Pope placed himself at the centre of the feudal system and increased the number of actions designed to ensure that the largest number of Catholic States fell under his sovereignty by using a custom developed in the 11th century according to which the Pope was the natural suzerain of all countries newly won over by the Catholic religion. But, most importantly (and this was what was applied to the Count of Toulouse, the suzerain of the Cathar region) was that, for the papacy, loyalty was no longer owed to those who were not loyal to the Catholic faith. The only reserve to this principle was the fact that the Pope declared that he recognised the rights on the matter of the leading lord, namely the suzerain of the lord concerned.

In order to succeed in its actions, whether strictly religious or political, the papacy had religious weapons at its disposal which it used in the fight against the Cathars, but which, after they proved to be ineffective, led to the armed crusade. These two weapons were excommunication and interdict.

Excommunication could be used at all levels of the Catholic hierarchy and, in the Middle Ages, it did not hesitate to do. It was possible to appeal to one's superiors against this sentence which consisted of depriving the person concerned of all aspects of religious life (entering the church and using the sacraments). Public reconciliation involved the punished person walking barefoot to the church to confess his transgressions and promising the required compensation. This put a term to a situation in which excommunicated people were considered to be accursed, avoided by family and friends and rejected by society.

Interdict had much more serious consequences because, decreed by the Pope against a lord, it put an end to any form of religious life in the territory affected. Churches were closed, bells were silenced, sacraments (except for christenings) were not administered and burials were conducted without any religious service.

Religious orders and Cathars

As we will see later when examining the course of events, the Church, in this case the Pope himself, was unable to rely on the local clergy alone to fight the Cathar heresy. It employed the support of two religious orders, one of which flourished as actions against the Cathars increased. This was the Dominican Order, but, prior to the creation of this, it was the Order of Cistercians, founded in 1098, the order to which Saint Bernard belonged in the 12th century. This Order grew rapidly and became known as the intransigent defender of the principles of the papacy and a sworn enemy of all those whom it saw as deviants to the most orthodox form of the religion. Compromise or understanding was not to be expected from the Cistercians engaged in the fight against the Cathars.

Pope Innocent III excommunicating the Albigensians and calling for a crusade against the heretics (1209).
Extract from *Les Grandes Chroniques de France*, manuscript from 1335. AKG-Images. London, British Library.

Saint Bernard, abbot of Clairvaux. The Cistercian Order, to which Saint Bernard belonged, played a leading role in the organisation of the crusade against the Albigensians.
Extract from *Le Livre d'Heures* by Etienne Chevalier, 1455.
AKG-Images. Chantilly, Musée Condé.

The Cistercian Order and the fight against the Cathars

The Cistercian Order was asked for two forms of assistance in the fight against the Cathars.

Firstly, preaching. This Order was created in 1098 and experienced rapid growth: 350 monasteries in 1153 and 495 in 1195. The preaching work demanded of Cistercian monks in the second half of the 12th century did not really suit them because they were trained in meditation and prayer and it proved to be a failure.

However, astonishingly, when considering this vocation of prayer, the work as pontifical legate and leader of men was more effective in view of the Pope's objectives and the Cistercian Order played a key role in leading the crusade against the Albigensians until the death of Simon de Montfort (1218). Their withdrawal was gradual and was almost completed during the royal forays (1224-1229). To this was added the activity of the Cistercian bishops: Guy, Abbot of Vaux-de-Cernay (Bishop of Carcassonne) and Fulk (Bishop of Toulouse).

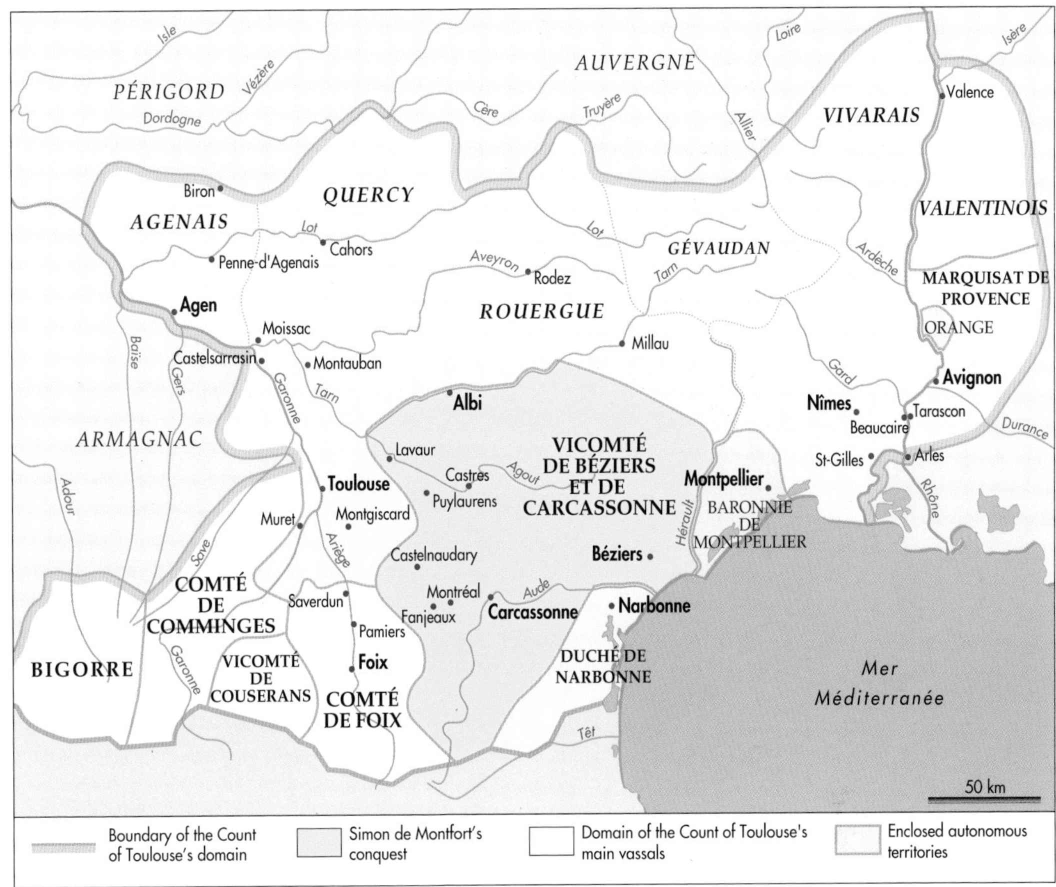

The domains of the Count of Toulouse and of his main vassals. The boundaries are approximate in view of the highly complex and interwoven nature of feudal relationships.

As for the Dominican Order, it was involved directly in the creation and functioning of the "Holy Inquisition", therefore intimately linked to the repression of the Cathar heresy.

Political aspects

We have seen above that the Cathar tragedy may not be reduced to religion alone because strong material interests – mechanisms of the feudal system, the development of theocracy and the means at the papacy's disposal – meant that any form of armed intervention to solve the growing problem of heresy in the specific environment of the Languedoc region would necessarily have repercussions on the political structures of this region and the neighbouring States (although this term should be used with caution when referring to the 13th century).

Three political players were involved in the Cathar affair: the County of Toulouse of course, but also its powerful southern neighbour, namely the Kingdom of Aragon, and the large emerging nation of the Kingdom of France, which continued to grow beyond its centre in Ile-de-France.

The County of Toulouse

Because the Count and County of Toulouse were at the heart of the events of the Cathar tragedy, it is necessary to analyse their situation and recall which power they represented.

In simple terms, it can be said that this was a powerful vassal of the King of France in a region with an original culture different from the one recognised at that time by the northern "French": language, economy, way of life, legal reference system (written Roman law), all of which made Occitan, Languedoc, a world very different from the birthplace of the kingdom of France.

The Archbishops' Palace and the Town of Narbonne.

It is through feudal ties that it is easiest to understand the complexity of the factors weighing on the unfolding of events. The list of titles itself is revealing: the Count of Toulouse was also the Duke of Narbonne and the Marquis of Provence; these, and other more minor titles, made him vassal to the King of France, the King of England and the King of Aragon; he was also, as a result of a historical and feudal curiosity, the vassal of the Emperor of Germany: Arles was still, theoretically, part of the Imperial Germanic empire, the vestige of a kingdom which has since disappeared. Also, as often happened in the feudal system, the family of the Counts of Toulouse was related by marriage to the royal households of France, England and Aragon.

In geographical terms, the authority (feudal, which limited its scope) of the Count of Toulouse spanned the regions of Agen, Quercy, Rouergue, Albi, Comminges, Carcassès and the County of Foix.

We have just spoken about feudal authority, but, in actual fact, in order to understand certain aspects, and not the least important, of the Cathar affair, it is necessary to remember the sometimes scattered nature of feudal authority.

Compared to his suzerains, the Count of Toulouse had great autonomy owing mainly

The domains of the County of Toulouse

At the time of the start of the crusade against the Cathars, the County of Toulouse was a very powerful regional power, although, sometimes, the complex nature of feudal ties meant that the vassals' dependency links were relatively flexible.

What were these domains? From East to West, the Marquisate of Provence, Vivarais, the Barony of Montpellier, Gévaudan, Rouergue, the Viscountcy of Béziers and of Carcassonne, the Duchy of Narbonne, the County of Foix, the Viscountcy of Couserans, the County of Comminges, Quercy and the Agenais, and, of course, the region of Toulouse.

< Seal of Raymond VI, Count of Toulouse.
Archives Nationales, Paris.

Raymond VII, Count of Toulouse, whose seal can be seen here, was forced to surrender after the intervention of the King of France and to hand over his domain.
Archives Nationales, Paris.

to geographical remoteness. This was particularly the case with the King of England and even the King of France. The situation was more complex with the King of Aragon because the vassals of the Count of Toulouse were also the vassals of the King of Aragon, who, furthermore, held direct control over Montpellier and Millau.

In terms of his vassals, the Count of Toulouse sometimes found himself in an uncomfortable position. The family of Trencavel (in Béziers) held the regions of Carcassès, Albi and were vassals of the King of Aragon. Also, the Counts of Foix never recognised the authority of the Counts of Toulouse.

In this Occitan feudal system, the clergy occupied its own place, its full place it could be said, because confusion between the temporal and the spiritual was one of the factors which facilitated the success of the Cathar heresy, especially since the bishops barely acknowledged the papacy's instructions and observations. Along with the mechanisms of the feudal system, the Count of Toulouse, in comparison to the King of France, controlled towns which were going to play an important role in Cathar history.

Landscape of Corbières.

A musician playing the vielle with a bow. In the so-called musicians' room of Puivert Castle.
Photo J. Debru.

Occitan

Etymologically, "oc" means "yes", which explains the expression lingua occitania meaning the "country where we say oc for yes". It appears that this expression was used regularly from the end of the 13th century at fairs in Champagne, in opposition to langue d'oil ("yes") used in the north and the centre of the Kingdom of France.
The two languages come from Latin but have different variations according to the so-called Barbarian invasions. With the region's incorporation into the Kingdom of France, the use of Occitan declined in favour of the langue d'oil which was used by the royal administration. At the time of the Albigensian crusade, the differences between the two languages were very pronounced.

Troubadours playing at a celebratory feast.
Extract from Regnault de Montauban, manuscript from 1470.
AKG-Images. Paris, Bibliothèque de l'Arsenal.

Mediano Church in Aragon.

Unlike in "France", Roman law had not disappeared. Its principles and even a large part of its practical measures were still very much alive and formed the basis of jurisdiction. Towns were managed by *capitouls* or consuls elected by the town's nobles and bourgeoisie. There was legal and de facto equality between nobles and the bourgeoisie in urban areas. However, in the 13th century, at the time of the Cathar tragedy, the prosperity of these towns was based on trade and exchanges with the outside world, which encouraged the dissemination of new ideas. The towns, rich from the profits of trade, often took advantage of this wealth to buy the rights of impoverished nobles (often, setting out on a crusade led to the sudden impoverishment of this class of gentry). This was why, in his own town, the powerful Count of Toulouse only had a very limited authority which, very often, was questioned by the organisations around which the town's life was structured. We will see that the lack of energy over the Cathar question for which he was so often reproached was not just a result of his indecision or of his undeclared sympathy for the heretics.

The existence of a specific language, Occitan, (langue d'oil being the language of the North) and the taste for the themes sung by the troubadours were also a factor, shall we say, of the entire region's complicity when faced with the intervention of foreign forces, for example of pontifical origin.

The Kingdom of Aragon

Aragon was one of the players in the Cathar problem and, at certain times, it played a major role in that its direct intervention in events was able to tilt the results one way (in favour of the Count of Toulouse) or the other (in favour of the anti-Cathar crusaders). Therefore, it is interesting to give a short presentation of this kingdom.

Until 1164, Aragon was just a small kingdom on the other side of the Pyrenees. It was its merger with the County of Barcelona which allowed it to intervene on an international level.

Pyrénées Orientales, views from the Font-Romeu wayside cross over Cerdagne.

Merger may be too strong a word because it was a complex political territory inside which the various components maintained their independence. It was the fact that these belonged to one sole sovereign which ensured its homogeneity. In all events, the union with the Count of Barcelona led to the start of strong and durable geographical expansion.

In terms of the region of interest to us, namely the area stretching from Toulouse to the Pyrenees, a genuine historical "inversion" occurred. Until about 1150, the Kings of France had succeeded in maintaining the principle of a certain feudal-based authority over Catalonia, which formed a border point in the kingdom of Charlemagne.

The increase in power of Aragon-Catalonia gave rise to the idea of a State stretching from the Ebre to Provence with the Garonne as its northern border. This State could have had a certain unity in terms of language (Occitan), culture and law (Roman law). Shortly

before 1100, Béarn and Bigorre passed under the influence of Aragon. In 1170, Béarn became a vassal of Aragon, whose King, Alfonso II, inherited at the same time feudal rights belonging to the Count of Barcelona: County of Provence, Roussillon. Two marriages by Counts of Barcelona also provided the brother of the King of Aragon with feudal authority over Carcassonne, Narbonne and Cerdagne.

It is easy to understand why this expansion was a concern for the Counts of Toulouse who sought to form alliances. Aragon did likewise and, in 1158, concluded an agreement with Henry II of England, also lord of Aquitaine. This agreement led to an Anglo-Catalonian army invading the County of Toulouse. Asked for assistance, the King of France stopped the army and saved the Count of Toulouse.

When the war against the Cathars broke out, the ambitions of Aragon did not change as we will see. However, the practical methods of Aragon policy did change. In 1204, Raymond VI

Pyrénées Orientales, Conflent and the Canigou Mountain.

The Pyrenees, emblematic landscape of the Cathar tragedy.

of Toulouse married a sister of Peter II of Aragon and signed a full alliance treaty with the only reserves concerning feudal law: to not intervene against the King of Castilla for Peter II, or against the King of France, the King of England and the Emperor for Raymond VI.

The position of the King of France

When considering the result of the Cathar affair, namely the complete incorporation of the County of Toulouse into the Kingdom of France, it is tempting to presuppose an intentional policy by the Kings of France. But this would be too simplistic and is something which is belied by the course of events.

From 1180 to 1270, three Kings succeeded each other on the throne: Philip II, called Augustus (because he was born in August) who reigned from 1180 to 1223, his son Louis VIII (1223-1226) and finally Louis IX known as Saint Louis (1226-1270).

Philip Augustus eluded the persistent requests of the papacy several times to incite and lead a crusade against the "Albigensians".

Peter II of Aragon, the Catholic (1177-1213)

He became King of Aragon in 1196 on the death of his father Alfonso II. It was he who put a stop to the offensive of the Almohad dynasty in Spain and instituted the start of the Reconquista, which explains his nickname the Catholic, mainly as a result of his victory at the Battle of Las Navas de Tolosa in 1212.

Dissolute, extravagant and a lover of the literature of the troubadours, he was a remarkable fighter and a very shrewd politician. This also led him to act very firmly against the heretics (Edict of Girona in 1198 which repeated the measures already decreed by his father in 1194) and to oppose by force the armed intervention of the Church.

But his main political goal was to succeed with the conclusive expansion of Aragon to the north of the Pyrenees; this led to the Battle of Mort, where he met his death.

This may be explained not by any sympathy for the heretics, but by the fact that his main preoccupation was the fight against the House of Plantagenet (namely the dynasty of the English throne represented by Richard Lionheart and John Lackland) to recover French fiefs. His personal relationships with the papacy were not very good since he had been excommunicated and the kingdom of France had been placed under interdict because of the Church's repudiation of his wife Ingeborg of Denmark, whom the King later reconciled with in 1213. Yet, this did not prevent the Pope from suggesting in a letter in 1204 to Philip Augustus that he should incorporate Occitania into France.

However, his son Louis VIII took part in the first and second crusades against the Cathars. It was Louis IX, known as Saint Louis, who ensured that the region was incorporated gradually into the kingdom from 1250 before it finally became part of France in 1271 (on the death of Alphonse of Poitiers, Saint Louis' brother and husband of the only daughter of the Count of Toulouse) in the reign of Phillip III, the Bold, Saint Louis's son who succeeded him in 1270 and who died in 1285 in Perpignan on his return from a campaign against the King of Aragon.

gl'a eius. gl'a q'si unigeniti a p
atre. Plenu' gracie et u'itatis.
Joh's testimoniu' p'hibet de ip'o. E
t clamabat dicens. hic est q'm
dixi. qui post me uenturus est. a
te me fact' est. q' p'or me erat.
erat. Et de plenitudine eius n
os omn's accep'im' gr'am p' gr'a. q'a
lex per moysen data est. gr'a e
u'itas p' ih'm x'pm facta est.

Ds em
uegut
d'nault
d'u. ed
nar u
os. ede
nar la
sorda na
nir de
sca' glisa precel' s'uisi. epdo. e
penedensia. d'tuit li n'ri pecat li
q'l auem fait. uidis. n'pessatz. m
obratz. del n're naissement ent' fi na

Adorem deu e manifeste tuit
li n're pecat. e las n'ras mo
utas greus ofensios. d'aqels gar
danit del paire celestial. e del onora
S. esp'it. e dels onoratz sanhs au
angels. e dels onoratz S. apostols.
P la oro. e p la fe. e p la saluatio d
tuit li diters gliosses creiatas. e
dels bonauiatz ourmitz aceiors e
dels fizels enauiro elar. e duat
nos. S. senhor qui nos p'domet tot go
q'a nos pecam. b'ndicite parcite nob'.

Qvar moutz soles n'res pe
catz els q'ls nos ofende' ani
cadia. p'muit ep'dia. e'parau
la. e obra e segon cossirer. ab uo
lontat e senes uolontat. E p' p
la n'ra uolontat. la q'l d'nat nos
apertan les malignus esp'itz en
las cars que uestem. b'ndici
te parcite nobis. HH

Mdir ai c'ula sca' paraula
d'd'u nos e'nba el. S. a

The Cathar religion

Describing even briefly the content of Cathar religion must be done in a spirit of great humility because there are many difficulties to overcome.

The first question concerns what do we have to rely on to describe this religion? We do not have any general documents and the very few sources are of dubious reliability. It is true that there are chronicles describing one or other aspect of the ideas or practices of Cathar religion, but it must be remembered that their authors were not always eye witnesses to the events or, often, were openly hostile to Cathar philosophy. The most available source is the mass of records from the interrogations by the Inquisitors, although it is necessary to ignore the objection raised by some purists for whom the elements of faith and the rites described by the victims of these interrogations (often under conditions which compromised the spontaneity of what was being said) describe a situation of "degenerate" Catharism because they are taken relatively late in time. Also it should be pointed out that such records do not help to convey a summarised version of the events.

There is, however, a third, normally, more reliable source, but one which is relatively fragmented. This concerns some of the documents on Cathar rituals which have been handed down to us. As their name suggests, these are not summarised presentations of the faith or the catechisms containing questions and answers about them, but, rather, an approach to the ways in which these were practised. At that time, there was a large number of these small practical manuals available, although, of course, most of them have since disappeared, burned by the Inquisitors.

On this point, it is interesting to note a specific trait of Cathar preachers which partly helps to explain their success. Largely ahead of the position of Luther in this field, these preachers used the common language in their work, namely Occitan, the language understood by all, whereas

< Cathar ritual.
This first page of a Cathar ritual is very moving because only very few authentic Cathar documents remain.
Bibliothèque Municipale de Lyon, Ms P. A 36, f° 236. Photo Didier Nicole.

The bell tower of the Cistercian Abbey of Fontfroide seen from inside the cloister.

Catholic preaching was in Latin, a language which practically none of the population understood.

Of the three Cathar rituals which have survived the flames and the passage of time, two are written in Occitan and one in Latin. The most surprising is a prayer (a Lord's Prayer) in Occitan which comes from the County of Foix and which is thought to date from the 13th century. It was found in 1950 and was published in 1967.

In view of the limited amount of material available, two questions spring immediately to mind. The first is whether there actually was a complete and homogenous doctrine and, secondly, what the Cathar "church" actually consisted of, if there really ever was one.

It is true that there was no established body with monasteries and parish churches, but it has been proved that a form of hierarchy did exist. At the bottom was the believer, namely the one who was joined to the religion by the melioramentum (see later). The believer was not yet part of the church, but he had promised to join it before his death and, therefore, was already linked to it through secrecy. The actual religious hierarchy was made up of novices, deacons and above them were the bishops. It has been proved that there were Cathar bishops but little is known about their role and the only reliable document (because what has been said on this subject by people interrogated by the Inquisitors should be read with great caution) are the acts of a Cathar Council held in 1167 at Saint-Félix Lauragais (in the present-day Haute-Garonne). At that time, there was a Cathar bishop in Albi and in view of the development of the Cathar faith in the region, it was decided to divide up this bishopric and to establish three other bishops in Toulouse, Agen and Carcassonne.

The cloister of Béziers Cathedral.

The Cathar Lord's Prayer (translation from Occitan)

This prayer was said in Occitan every evening by a farmer from Ariege who died in 1947 and who did not know the Catholic Lord's Prayer. It had been transmitted orally and in secret over the centuries.

"Holy Father, Fair God of Good Spirits, you who are never wrong, who never lies, who never roams, who never doubts that we will not die in the world of the Unknown God (Evil), because we are not of this world and he is not one of ours, teach us to know and to love what you love.

The Pharisee tempters are at the gates of Heaven and prevent those from entering who wish to do so, while they themselves do not wish to go there. That is why I pray to the Holy Father of Good Spirits. He has the power to save souls and, I give thanks to the Good Spirits, for making them germinate and blossom. Yet, among the good ones, he also gives life to evil ones. He will act thus for as long as there are good souls in this world, until there is not one more of his own (his young ones) on earth. His own are those who

Depiction of Hell.
15th century manuscript, extract from the *City of God* by Saint Augustine. Bibliothèque Nationale, Paris, Ms fr. 28, f° 249 v°.

come from the seven kingdoms, who fell from Paradise, when Lucifer drew them to him by declaring that God was fooling them because he only allowed them GOOD. The infinitely false Devil promised them GOOD and EVIL. He assured them that he would give them women to love, that they would command, that some of them would be kings, counts or emperors, that with one bird they could capture another, with one beast, they could seize another.

All those who obey the Devil will descend below and may, as they wish, do GOOD and EVIL, the same as god in heaven; he added that it would be best to be below where they could choose between GOOD and EVIL, whereas God would only allow GOOD.

Thus, some climb on a glass sky and rise to the heavens, others fall and meet their death.

So God descended from heaven with twelve apostles and he brought forth – gave birth to – Saint Mary. (To save those who are good – Good Christians)."

Extract from *Rituels Cathares* by Michel Gardère, La Table Ronde, 1996, p. 89-91.

Saint-Michel Church in Castelnaudary.

> Cross of Saint-Michel Church in Castelnaudary.

It is interesting to note that at this Council, Cathars from overseas were also present (a point which raises a second question), in particular a person who appears in the acts to have held a position of authority, namely the Cathar Bishop of Constantinople.

So what can be said about the origins and the relationships of Catharism with other countries? Much has been written on this subject, and people have sought to make connections with Hindu doctrine and sun worship, etc. What is certain (and the presence of a Cathar Bishop from Constantinople in Languedoc in 1167 is proof of this) is that, in the 10th century a body of doctrine very similar to the Cathars developed in the Balkans, and more specifically in Macedonia with Brother Bogomil, but it did not identify itself with the Cathars.

The Bogomils spread their influence from Macedonia to the Peloponnese, to the present-day Turkey and Bosnia, where their principles became the religion of State in around 1180. All of this was destroyed by the Ottoman invasion in the 14th and 15th centuries.

Having said that, what can we say with certainty about Cathar doctrine and rites? Since Catharism emerged within a deeply Christian, Catholic society, it is best to try and understand how this doctrine and these rites differed from the commonly established religion in Languedoc.

Christian doctrine is essentially monotheist with the idea of an all-powerful and profoundly good God. But, ever since the start of this religion, two key questions have been asked, which, over the centuries, have led to vehemently contrasting replies being given at regular intervals:

— If God is all-powerful, how can man ensure his salvation? Does he have access to a free arbitrator? Is everything defined from birth, or is it possible to change one's destiny? And, if this is the case, is there not a limit to the omnipotence of God?

— Good and Evil coexist in everyday life, if God is good and all-powerful why does he allow Evil to exist?

It is this last question which lies at the heart of Catharism, with Protestantism and Jansenism, having developed from an attempt to answer the first question.

For Cathars, there could be no doubt: the origin of the existence of Evil in the everyday world was a result of the fact that there was not one God, but two, one Good, the other Evil. This is what is called Dualism. It was the fight between God and Lucifer that led to the parallel existence of two Gods, but who were they?

The Good God reigned over the skies and created the spirits. The Evil God reigned over the land and created things that were visible, including humans in their carnal form, while human souls were spirits created by the Good God. The number of souls was defined at the time of Creation, and each soul could have nine bodies. At the last incarnation (the ninth), a person would cross into Paradise or descend into Hell. Therefore, metempsychosis may have been part of Cathar doctrine.

However, this last point is not completely clear because some preachers rejected

Detail from the Last Judgement, fresco in Sainte-Cécile Cathedral in Albi.
Photo Richard Nourry.

the very idea of Eternal Hell. For them, Hell was life on earth. What was important was the fact that the soul was seen as a celestial creation, the emanation of the Good God, a small part of the divine substance which had been imprisoned in flesh, a diabolical invention. Nowadays, in our deeply unchristian world where the notion of religion in the Christian, Catholic sense of the term has lost much of its meaning and influence, it is difficult to understand how deeply this doctrine must have disturbed medieval thinking.

In order to fully understand the almost revolutionary nature of Cathar doctrine, let us attempt to draw up a brief list of what was rejected.

In religious terms, Cathar doctrine rejected everything about redemption from Evil through Christ being sent down to earth. Sacraments were also rejected, including communion, as was the worship of the Cross, because the coming of Christ was nothing but an illusion and a deception, and the body of Christ was created by the Devil (the Bad God). The Christian clergy preached a catechesis of fear based on the idea that if their followers were not forgiven, Hell awaited them after their death. Cathars were certain to find (or return to) the radiant world of Good after their death on the sole condition that they join the Cathar faith.

The simplicity of Cathar doctrine (compared to Christian dogma) can be seen in the

Peyrepertuse Castle, a magnificent fortified site.

Peyrepertuse Castle.

rites. These are known from the documents referred to earlier and from the declarations made to the Inquisitors.

Cathars considered traditional Christian baptism with water to be of no value and replaced it with the idea that two different processes were possible, namely attaining the state of "perfection" or being baptised in the final hours of one's life.

Simple believers, namely those who had not yet received consolamentum, practised the rite of melioramentum in the same way as the Perfects (this was the term used by the Inquisitors and corresponds to the Occitan term milhoirer). This was both a sign of respect, because the Perfect embodied the Holy Spirit, and the expression of a request: the believer wanted to be blessed. It involved three genuflections (some texts talk of prostration) followed by a kiss of peace (especially when the believer was carrying out this rite for the very first time). However, once Cathar practices started to be monitored, a more discreet procedure was used, for example, a simple nod of the head.

The consolamentum ("consolement" in Occitan), namely consolation, had much

The knights' fresco in the Count's Castle of Carcassonne.
Photo J. Debru.

wider meaning and scope. It was a proper baptism which allowed a person to attain the state of being a "Perfect". This may have been carried out, as we have just mentioned, under two different circumstances.

The first case was for a believer to attain the state of being Perfect, which could be compared with that of being an ordained priest. Catharism employed the novitiate system which, among other things, contributed to making it very innovative compared to Christian religion. Women were not excluded from the novitiate which lasted for different periods of time (at least one year). During this period, the novice had to comply with the ritual abstinence, something we will examine later, and learn certain texts by heart (without necessarily having to know how to read), particularly the first chapter of the Gospel according to John. The ceremony included an exhortation by the officiant (a confirmed "Perfect") to the believer on the theme of Our Father in order that he could repent his sins and take his vows. The officiant then baptised him by laying on his hands, depicting the arrival of the consolamentum in the believer's soul.

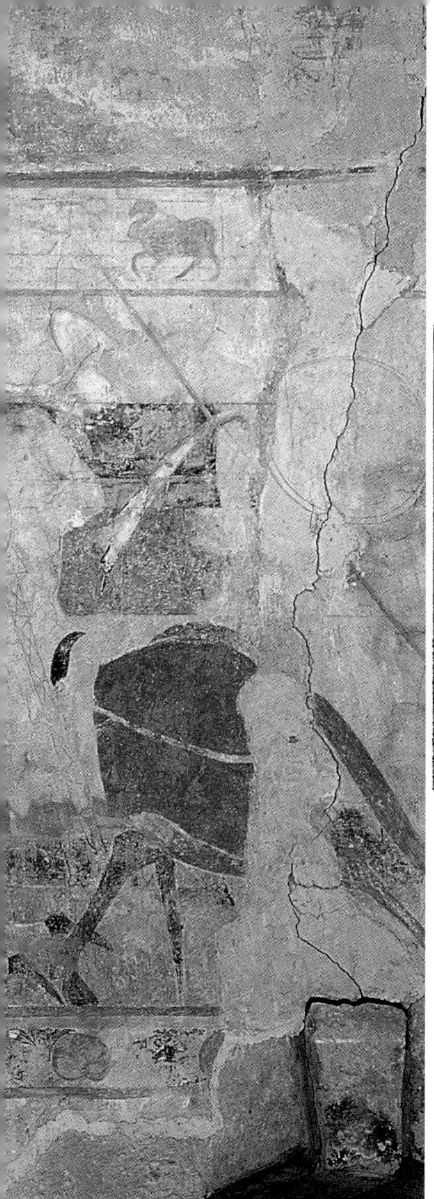

Three discoid stelae in the Count's Castle of Carcassonne.
Photo J. Debru.

This "ordination" applied to women as much as to men. When it involved married people, the other member of the couple was required to give his or her consent, or even better, to ask to receive the consolamentum as well.

This is easy to understand in view of the fact that abstinence and chastity were required from the Perfect in all aspects of daily life. He had to abstain from any form of fat, with the exception of oil and fish, which meant no meat, eggs, milk, dairy products or cheese. Justifications of these rules tend to vary: the products were forbidden because they were the result of the fornication of beasts, whereas fish was not forbidden because it was created in water; blood was the channel through which metempsychosis worked, which was why all animals were rejected apart from fish which, according to Cathars, did not have any blood. Here again, the fact that the Cathars' declarations to the Inquisitors were not completely reliable generate a certain amount of uncertainty. It should be noted that wine was not forbidden.

In addition to the rules of abstinence, the Perfect had to follow three forty-day fasts a year. During these periods, the fast was even stricter (bread and water) in the first and final week, as well as on every Monday, Wednesday and Friday.

In general, food preparation had to follow very meticulous rules designed to avoid any violation of the rules of abstinence. Perfects had to live in pairs, own their own cooking implements, wash them five times, etc. It is easy to imagine the difficulties encountered when the Perfects were hunted down by the Inquisition.

The rite of consolamentum was also carried out on another occasion, namely just

The so-called Bogomil Christ provides proof of a link between the Cathar religion and the heretics established in the present-day country of Bulgaria.
It is found near the Church of Les Cassès, north of Castelnaudary.
Photo J. Debru.

before death when a Perfect baptised a believer in his final hours, thus ensuring the absolution of his sins and his salvation, and also allowing him to not have to assume the oppressive duties of the Perfect.

The actual procedure combined a form of melioramentum and consolamentum. The sick person had to kneel to make a promise to adhere to the faith, make a donation (symbolic if necessary) to the Church, declare to agree to the rules of abstinence and received "consolation" from the Prefect by the laying on of hands.

There is much debate among scholars about the conditions of sick or dying people after receiving the consolamentum. This concerns the question of the endura, namely the period during which the sufferer remained without food while awaiting death. The endura was the penitential fast observed by Christ during the forty days he spent in the desert.

In real terms, the following remarks can be made. Usually, in extremis, as coma approached or as he lost consciousness, the sick person received a basic sacrament which made him a Perfect and ensured his salvation. However, in some cases, people survived meaning that they had to follow the life of a Perfect.

Nevertheless, some people, after reading certain texts, believed that the person was obliged to commit suicide by starvation and, if necessary, that he was assisted by his entourage. But, no facts were found by the Inquisitors to support this theory.

In order to understand the Cathar drama, we must now question the consequences of this doctrine and its rites on social life. In general, in application of the fundamental belief that the visible world was thoroughly diabolical, Cathar doctrine rejected the feudal system, the payment of taxes, the lords' or royal system of justice, etc. But, a difference should be made between the case of the simple believer and the Perfect who could neither lie nor take an oath. The fact that he could not take an oath prevented the usual application of the rules of feudal society and the obligation to tell the truth led to some very serious consequences during interrogations of the Perfects. The outright refusal to kill was also contrary to the functioning of the feudal system. This also applied to animals (which may have received a celestial soul) and was something that helped to identify Perfects, although it should be noted that it did not apply to cold-blooded animals (fish, reptiles). They also rejected civil justice with Perfects being required to solve disputes through amicable arbitration.

It is not possible to give a detailed list here of the social practices which contradicted society at that time, but, in order to conclude this very rapid summary, mention should be made of the Perfect's obligation to carry out manual work, an important difference from the Christian clergy: they could eat what they had earned.

Ultimately, Cathar religion was characterised by a homogenous set of doctrinal principles and rites. There was a great divide between Catharism, the feudal system and the basics of Christian religious life, something which begs the question of whether the spread of Catharism might not have led to social revolt. But, there was never revolt because the Cathars did not believe that it was possible to act on Evil, therefore, it was not possible to change the world and to establish fair and good social laws. There was wide-scale agreement between the Cathars on this point despite the fact that all layers of society were involved in this movement. Records of interrogations are very clear on this point because Cathars were to be found among the gentry, traders, craftsmen, notaries, doctors, farmers, etc, in short, in all the social classes.

Violence did not come from the Cathars, but, as we will see, was the result of Rome's wish to eliminate this movement by using the armed force of the "French" feudal world from north of the Loire.

Medieval celebrations in Carcassonne.

The unfolding of events

The end of what some refer to as the "Cathar era" is often dated to the fall of Montségur Castle and the burning at the stake of about 210 people, namely in 1243. In actual fact, the very last Perfect was arrested and identified and burnt at the stake in 1321. Quéribus Castle, the indisputable Cathar refuge, fell in 1255.

The start of the Cathar heresy is much more uncertain and even unknown. Documents help us to confirm that the ideas of the Manichean principle and divine dualism (Good and Evil) were present in Western Europe at the start of the 11th century. The relationship with Bulgarian Bogolism has not been confirmed, but, in 1022, ten canons preaching ideas similar to those of the Cathars were burnt at the stake in Toulouse. However, we do know that the Second Council of Toulouse in 1119 condemned the heresy already widespread in the region in similar terms to those of the Second Council of the Lateran, applying them to the Albigensians alone.

The events unfolded around several periods: at the end of the 11th century and at the start of the 12th century. This involved pacific preaching, although, already in 1180, a Papal legate had requested a military crusade. The assassination of a Papal legate in 1208 speeded up events resulting in a first crusade between 1209 and 1224, followed by a second from 1226 to 1229. As we have mentioned earlier, Catharism was almost completely eradicated by 1243 and 1255.

The situation at the start of the 13th century

The spread of Cathar ideas

From the second half of the 12th century, the strong development of Cathar ideas brought to the attention of the Church and, above all of the papacy, the fact that Albigensian feudal lords were not hunting down heretics, who already had a large network of accomplices. In 1163, the Council of Tours noted that Saint Bernard's preaching in Languedoc in around 1145 had had no effect and led to talk of "a damnable heresy" which "has spread little by little over Gascony and other provinces" and which "has already infected a very large number of people". This acknowledgement of failure gave strength to the heated debate in Lombers (near Albi) in 1165 between Catholic priests and "Good Men"

< Saint Dominic burns Albigensian documents. Auto-da-fés were a common procedure used to eradicate heresy.

Painting by Pedro Berruguete (1495). AKG-Images/Erich Lessing. Madrid, Prado Museum.

The village of Saissac and the Lauragais plain stretching to the Pyrenees.

Bottom:
Stained glass window depicting Saint Dominic in the house dedicated to him in Fanjeaux.

Sculpture of Saint Dominic in the house devoted to him in Fanjeaux.

(namely Cathar priests, those whom the Inquisition would later refer to as "Perfects", see inset). On a number of points, the Cathars supported very orthodox viewpoints, either out of secrecy, or because Cathar doctrine developed at a later date. The dispute concerned the Cathars refusal to take an oath. All the prelates present accused the Good Men of heresy, with, in their eyes, their refusal to swear allegiance to the Christian faith providing proof of this.

The renewed growth in Cathar ideas led to the organisation of a Cathar Council in Saint-Félix Lauragais (between Toulouse and Revel) in 1167. This was a real challenge for the Catholic Church because the Assembly was presided over by a heretic bishop from Constantinople by the name of Niketas. This man's presence has generated much debate. For some, Catharism had not come to France from the Balkans - quite the contrary - but had been established in the Balkans by the Franks or crusaders from the Rhine Valley. The question is still a controversial one. The very existence of the Cathar Council, and, therefore, of the decisions it took, is also sometimes disputed. Yet, some of the decisions taken were very significant and the related document recounts the decision to establish three bishops (Cathar) in Toulouse, Carcassonne and Agen.

The position of the civil authorities

This Cathar Council (if it really did take place) was a blatant and provocative violation of a request made by the Church to the civil authorities that feudal lords, firstly the Count of Toulouse and his main vassals, prevent meetings of heretics.

Why was the Count of Toulouse so passive? The explanation may be found in the content of the extremely worried letter sent by Raymond V to the General Chapter of the Cistercian Order (of which Saint Bernard had been a member) in September 1177.

This text is particularly interesting because it marks a turning point. The highest form of civil authority in the region, the Count of Toulouse, questioned the fact that several of his vassals were converting to heresy, casting doubt on the effectiveness of purely spiritual measures (interdict, anathema, etc.) and calling upon the assistance of the King of France, who, in turn, initiated the series of decisions leading to the bloody events which followed the start of the military campaign of the crusades in 1209.

But what about the clergy?

The powerlessness of the local clergy

Faced with the rise in power of the Cathar faith, the local clergy found itself powerless for several reasons.

The first, and most certainly the most important reason, was that the methods of preaching and the type of lives led by Cathar Perfects were much more effective than those of Catholic priests. The population, from the most humble to the most powerful, spoke the same language as the Cathars and the obstacles of the obscure Latin language spoken by a rare few did not exist. In intellectual terms, the abundance and the repetition of texts studied by the synods

The cloister of the Jacobins Church in Toulouse.

The situation in 1177 seen by the Count of Toulouse

This pestilential contagion of heresy has spread so much [...] that it has created discord among those who were united, dividing husband and wife, father and son, mother-in-law and daughter-in-law. Even those called to the priesthood have been corrupted by its infection. Ancient churches, formerly respected, have been abandoned and are falling into disrepair. Baptism is refused, the Eucharist is abhorred, penitence is scorned, the creation of man and the resurrection is denied; all the Church's sacraments have been wiped out and even – such sacrilege! – it is said that there are two principles.

As for myself, armed with one of the two holy glaives, who confesses to be the avenger of the divine anger and the minister of God, I search in vain for a means to put a stop to such great evil. I acknowledge that I do not have the adequate forces to succeed with such a huge and difficult affair, because even the most noble in my land have already been infected by the evil of infidelity and are followed by a multitude of people who have abandoned the faith. I dare not and am unable to undertake any action.

Therefore, I humbly beg for your assistance, your council and your prayers in order to eradicate this heresy. Understand that its venom has penetrated so deeply that it may only be eradicated by the power of God and by his raised fist. And, since we know that the authority of the spiritual glaive is powerless to destroy such a perversion, it must be attacked by the severity of the real glaive. That is why I ask the Lord King of France to visit our country, convinced that his presence will help to uproot such great evil. While he is here, I will open the towns to him, deliver the villages and castles of his choosing, I will show him where the heretics are, and, when he requires it, I will assist him until my own blood is spilt, in order to exterminate all the enemies of Jesus Christ."

Extract from the letter he sent to the General Chapter of the Order of Cîteaux published by M. Roquebert in L'Epopée Cathare, tome II, Privat, 1995, p. 83-84.

As M. Roquebert rightly points out, the Count of Toulouse unintentionally triggered the mechanism leading to the crusade and the accompanying massacres.

(meetings of a diocese's priests organised by the bishop) on the pressing need to raise the level of instruction among the clergy clearly shows that, on the one hand, this was a serious and widespread problem and, that decisions on this matter were not put into force because it was something which was repeated constantly. The Perfects' evocation of the principles of Christianity was better understood than the rules pronounced by Rome.

Saint Francis appearing before Franciscan monks in Arles (1295).
Fresco in the Church of Saint-Francis of Assisi.
AKG-Images/Stefan Diller.

Eyewitness accounts and studies on this subject show that very few of the frontline members of the clergy, namely the priests and vicars, were able to teach the basics of traditional Christian doctrine to their flock. Preaching in everyday language was not very common, despite the fact that, aware of the dangers presented by the sole use of Latin texts, the Councils (meetings of bishops organised by the Pope), and the synods strongly recommended it. All of this explains why the clergy turned to preaching orders (Franciscans and Dominicans).

The intrusion of preaching monks into everyday religious life was not without incident and this conflict between priests and monks did not help the fight against the Cathars. However, the reasons for their disagreement were not just about methods of action, but also about their way of life. The term mendicant orders offers an insight into this problem with their members wanting to live from charity alone without having to rely on the traditional system.

Every parish church was seen as a spiritual responsibility and a source of revenue. Tithes were paid to the clergy: one sheaf of wheat or cereal out of every ten, eleven or twelve depending on the case, was taken from the field during harvest. The same applied, although not in all parishes, to animals. For simplicity's sake, during the Middle Ages, these tithes were converted gradually into cash payments. Refusal to pay (whether in kind or in cash) or fraud could result in excommunication.

To this was added the collection of "donations" by priests during liturgical festivals and religious ceremonies (christenings, weddings, funerals). Of course, the synods insisted that sacraments should be free of charge, but, in reality, they were almost always accompanied by an offering of a varying amount depending on the parish.

Foix Castle.
At the time of the Cathars, the Count of Foix represented a major economic and feudal power between the Count of Toulouse and the King of Aragon.
Photo J. Debru.

This may have led to a feeling of discontent among parishioners, emphasised by the fact that Perfects' doctrine and way of life were the complete opposite of those of the Catholic Church: great simplicity even austerity, the complete absence of any form of charge for the only sacrament administered (consolamentum) and high moral standards.

This final point must not be ignored because, without wishing to overemphasise its importance, it did play a role in the difficulties encountered by the clergy in halting the spread of Cathar doctrine. Although, at the start of the 13th century, the papacy had succeeded in eliminating cases of married priests (relatively frequent in the previous century), the fact that the Council of the Lateran (1215) continued to rail against priests living as man and wife and that reports by bishops often spoke of priests "sinning with their spiritual daughters" clearly show that the problem had not disappeared. Here again, a comparison with the way of life advocated and practised by Perfects did give Catharism a clear advantage.

The spread of Catharism among the gentry

The impact of Cathar ideas was not limited to the social classes attracted to the Perfects' way of life. One indisputable fact clearly highlights this point. This involved Esclarmonde of Foix's ordination as Perfect through the granting of the consolamentum. The ceremony, which took place in 1204, not only concerned this, the sister of the Count of Foix (therefore an important vassal of the Count of Toulouse), but also three other noblewomen. The congregation was said to have included fifty-seven people from the gentry, as well as members of the bourgeoisie.

This was not an isolated case and documents attest to the high number of members of the nobility joining the Cathar faith and choosing to become Perfects, as well as to the place occupied by women. This is not surprising when considering the entirely innovative nature of this religion which did not see women as inferior beings, unable to access the function of priestess, and was something completely in line with Occitan culture.

First external intervention

As we can see, the situation for the Catholic Church barely improved after the very worried letter sent by the Count of Toulouse to the Cistercian Order in 1177 and we will have to go back a few years to understand the direct impact of this letter, a genuine call for help. The King of France was Louis VII, and the King of England was Henry II. The second was the vassal of the first, but the situation was rather complicated because the marriage of Henry II to Eleanor of Aquitaine, who had been repudiated by Louis VII, made him a much more powerful lord than the King of France, with power over England and Aquitaine.

The divorce of Louis VII (1152).
Extract from *Chroniques de Saint-Denis*, 1325. London, British Library. AKG-Images.

The two kings could not ignore the letter from the Count of Toulouse, especially since it arrived at a time when, with the help of the papal legate in France, Peter of Pavia, they had just signed an agreement to put an end to a conflict resulting from this contradiction of power within the feudal system. They had to intervene because the Cathar heresy might affect the two kingdoms and also because the call for help came from one of their vassals and, according to feudal law, the suzerain had to provide help and protection to a vassal in difficulty. After analysis of the situation, and with the agreement of the Pope, the two kings decided to form a delegation which would spend time in the County of Toulouse between 1178 and 1181, and whose objective would be both religious (bringing heretics back to the faith) and slightly military (because the use of force by local lords, especially the Count of Toulouse, was clearly envisaged).

This delegation, under the authority of the legate Peter of Pavia, included several bishops and archbishops (Narbonne, Bourges, Poitiers and Bath in England), as well as the Abbot of Clairvaux, Henry of Marcy.

This three-year mission played an often underestimated role in how events were going to unfold. In history, events may occur unexpectedly or randomly, but, sometimes, a series of facts together are able to trigger an irreversible course of events. This was the case of Peter of Pavia's mission which, through the use of threats and informants, succeeded in identifying dedicated Cathar followers and preachers. The processes and procedures used were already the same as those of the Holy Inquisition which, legally speaking was created several years later.

Two affairs dealt with by this mission are significant. The first concerns the abjuration of Pierre Maurand, a bourgeois from Toulouse known to be a Cathar preacher. He denied being a heretic but, in accordance with

Cathar ethics, he refused to swear to it under oath, something which, following the medieval concept of the role of oath taking made him particularly suspect. Under interrogation, he rejected the theory of the presence of Christ in the bread and wine of the Eucharist. Finally, he decided to abjure the Cathar faith and took part in a ceremony of expiation with an undertaking to travel to Jerusalem and to spend forty days there at the service of pilgrims.

The other affair was in Castres and concerned two leading Cathar figures, the Bishop of Toulouse present at the Cathar Council of 1177 and his deputy. They had been expelled by the Count of Toulouse (which proves that he was already acting against the Cathars) and wanted this restriction to be lifted by the legate. The legate refused, but they were offered safe-conduct to Lavaur (in Tarn).

This first mission was followed by a second entrusted by the Pope to a new legate, Henry of Marcy, the Abbot of Clairvaux, whom he made cardinal for the services rendered during the first mission. The aim was to identify the two Cathar leaders hiding in Lavaur. Siege was laid to the town and the two Cathars were captured and tried, despite the opposition of their protector, Viscount Roger II Trencavel, who was forced to concede. The two heretics were allowed to live and, after abjuring, ended their days as canons. Repression had not yet reached the degree of savagery that it would after 1209.

The arrival of Pope Innocent III and the start of his action in the region

The situation changed noticeably with the election in 1198 of a new Pope, Innocent III, on the death of Celestine III. Immediately after his election, he made a call for arms against the heretics, and, at the same time, brought the Occitan clergy and preaching to heel. It took the assassination in 1208 of his legate, Pierre de Castelnau, for him to feel that the only remaining solution would be armed action, namely an actual crusade.

The Archbishops' Palace in Narbonne.

As we have already said, the greatest difficulty encountered by the Pope and the Catholic Church in fighting the Cathar heresy was the condition of the Occitan upper clergy. As long as they, for various reasons (way of life incompatible with Christian rules, lack of dynamism, tacit or real complicity with the heretics) did not really involve themselves in the fight, Cathar ideas would continue to spread, including among the lower rural clergy.

In terms of the secular clergy (the regular clergy being that of monasteries and abbeys), the region was organised into two archbishoprics (Narbonne and Auch) and several bishoprics (Toulouse, Cahors, Albi, Tarbes, Agen, Lodève, Comminges, Béziers, Carcassonne, etc.). It was the Archbishop of Narbonne who posed the greatest problem to the Pope and it took four years (from 1203 to 1207) for him to be dismissed, although there were many reasons to do so: accumulation of profits,

On the left of the picture, Pope Innocent III can be seen dispatching his ambassadors to France. On the right, Philip Augustus is seen receiving an ambassador sent by the Pope (1200).
Extract from *Les Grandes Chroniques de France*, manuscript from 1335. London, British Library. AKG-Images/British Library.

simony (the collection of money to confirm an election in a chapter), lack of control over the diocese (no Episcopal visits), etc. Archbishop Berenger used all the means available to him under canon law to delay his fate.

Also deposed by the Pope was the papal legate of the Bishop of Carcassonne (in 1211), Vence, Toulouse and Valence (in 1211). The Archbishop of Auch was forced to resign (1211), as were the Bishops of Viviers (in 1201) and Rodez (1211).

All this disciplinary work was accompanied by preaching work carried out by the legates, which continued to produce unsatisfactory results.

A new period of firmness was marked by the appointment of two legates at the end of 1203, Pierre de Castelnau and Raoul de Fontfroide. Their first action in December 1203 was to obtain an oath of loyalty to the Pope and the Church from the Consuls Capitouls and representatives of the population of Toulouse in order, in some respects, to overcome the Count of Toulouse's passiveness or lack of dynamism. The oath was taken but with a clear restriction to maintain and respect communal liberties (proof that Toulouse had a special status within the feudal system). Also, the oath did not oblige the town to pursue heretics by expelling them.

The arrival of Arnaud-Amaury and the assassination of Pierre de Castelnau (1204-1208)

Increasingly wishing to resolve the Cathar problem, in 1204 (the year when the crusaders of the fourth crusade sacked Constantinople, the Christian city which they were supposed to save!) Innocent III decided to place a supreme leader, Arnaud-Amaury, Abbot of Cîteaux, above the two legates already in place. Very quickly the

Abbot realised the difficulties of his mission and the Pope, wanting to support him, appointed the Bishop of Toulouse Folguet (or Folgue or Foulques or Fulk) from Marseilles, Abbot of the Cistercian Abbey of Thoronet. He became a fanatical hunter of Cathars.

At the same time (1206) a meeting was held in Montpellier which was going to have a strong influence on the course of events. A Spanish bishop and the sub-prior of his chapter, who had seen the state of the situation when in Toulouse in 1203, decided to stop in the city again while on another journey. These were Diègue d'Acibès, the Bishop of Osma, and the future Saint Dominic. These two Spaniards presented a new method of preaching to the legates, which, according to them, should replace the traditional method which had failed. They should fight using the same methods as those employed by the Cathars, meaning that they should approach the heretics in all humility and as simply as possible. The proposal was accepted and the two Spaniards and the legates (except for Arnaud-Amaury who had to take part in the general chapter of the Cistercian Order) set out on foot, begging for their food and sleeping under the stars, passing through Béziers and Carcassonne. The legate Pierre de Castelnau was forced to withdraw because he was exposed to the population's hostility.

The momentum created was acknowledged and in 1206 Innocent III decreed the generalisation of this new method of preaching. The following year, the two Spaniards founded a convent in Prouille for young women who had abandoned the Cathar faith. Seeking a debate with the Perfects, they organised a contradictory meeting in Montréal (1207), which lasted for two weeks. Naturally, the meeting did not lead to any conclusions, but it did show that the Pope's representatives were taking the initiative.

Further proof of this reversal was the excommunication by Arnaud-Amaury of Count Raymond VI in 1207, with an interdict placed on his land. In the eyes of the legate and the Pope, there were many reasons for this, but, the most important was the Count's lack of reaction to heresy and, particularly, his refusal to lead the armed crusade which would have been called a "league of peace" (a curious name in view of what followed).

This was the prelude to the crusade with the Pope, who had not received a reply from Philip Augustus, turning directly to his main vassals (for example the Duke of Burgundy or the Count of Champagne).

However, the start of 1208 marked the turning point which led to the loss of so many lives: Pierre de Castelnau was assassinated near Saint-Gilles (on the right bank of the River Rhone near Arles).

Crusaders and bishop setting out on the crusade (1200).
Illumination from 1310.
AKG-Images/Erich Lessing.

A war scene in Toulouse. Toulouse was a centre in the fight against Catharism.

Manuscript from 1296, extract from *Les Coutumes de Toulouse*. Bibliothèque Nationale, Paris, Ms lat. 9187, f° 33.

The first crusade against the Cathars (1209-1213)

The circumstances of, causes and responsibilities for this assassination are uncertain, and even the date is a subject of controversy: 14 or 15 January, or 14 or 15 February 1208. However, what is important is that the legate Arnaud-Amaury was going to use the opportunity to implicate the Count of Toulouse even further and launch "his" crusade.

Two points remained to be clarified before the invasion: to neutralise the Count of Toulouse in his region and to obtain the agreement of the King of France.

Neutralising the Count of Toulouse was easy. He was accused immediately of murder, although there was nothing to support this theory with the most valid argument against it being the fact that he had no reason to provoke the Pope in this manner, since all his previous behaviour involved equivocation. Anathema was initiated against him, but the most important thing was to ensure that he was unable to act against any future and immediate crusade. To do this, the Pope and legates (even if there were slight differences, and sometimes even major differences, between the ways in which the Pope and his legates acted) worked in two ways: after being sentenced, an offer of redemption, meaning public humiliation, with penitence, and an oath to take part in the crusade. This was carried out in June 1208 at Saint-Gilles, where the tomb of the assassinated legate was to be found. In return for "taking up the cross", Raymond VI automatically placed his person and his property under the protection of the papacy.

The other problem, the agreement of the King of France, was more difficult to solve. Philip Augustus continued to insist to the Pope (whom he replied to directly very rarely) that launching a crusade only made sense if the papacy undertook to protect the kingdom of France from attacks from the English and Germans (in this case one of the two pretenders to the Imperial throne). Do not forget that it was in 1214, with the victory of the Battle of Bouvines, that Philip Augustus eliminated the German threat and, at the same time, succeeded in driving back the English.

Detail from a stained glass window in Notre-Dame de Chartres dating from around 1250, in which a fully armed Simon de Montfort is depicted.
Bibliothèque Nationale, Paris, RES OA-9-FOL, f° 88.

Innocent III increased pressure on the King of France and his main vassals, but Philip Augustus would not relent. He did allow his vassals to take part in the crusade, but he did not participate in it himself (in 1216, his son Louis, the future Louis VIII, did) and, above all, he reminded the Pope of his main duty as suzerain of the Count of Toulouse. The Pope could not expropriate the Count if he had not been sentenced for heresy. In all cases, the crusade was organised without the support of the French King.

The events of this crusade took place within a feudal framework, meaning that the lords participated in it for forty days (ost), preferably during the summer months (so that there was maximum damage to crops). These troops of nobles were accompanied by a large number of armed men and servants, etc. All these people lived from the land, placing a heavy burden on those being invaded, not to mention the cost of the passage of soldiers, all the more prone to excess because they were unpaid and were aware of the hostility of those who, theoretically, they had come to free from heresy as well as the fact that – something not to be forgotten – the invaders and the invaded did not speak the same language because the crusaders came from Ile-de-France, Champagne, Burgundy and other areas where langue d'oil was spoken.

Under these conditions, and taking account of the religious fanaticism of both sides, it is not surprising that this crusade turned into a bloody and destructive foray. All the documents available underline its apocalyptic nature, and even if the figures are not very reliable, they only serve to exaggerate a reality which was fundamentally horrific.

Some of the participants in the first crusade

Major prelates: Archbishop of Sens, Bishops of Nevers, Clermont, Autun.
Major lords: Duke of Burgundy, Count of Nevers, Count of Bar-sur-Seine, Count of Geneva, Count of Valentinois, Count of Saint-Pol.
Minor lords: Simon de Montfort, Guillaume des Roches, Gaucher de Joigny, etc.
But, do not forget that:
- many of the lords who took part in the crusade remained anonymous;
- each one was accompanied by his own vassals, archers or crossbowmen, and soldiers;
- the ost system meant a constant flow of departures and arrivals.

The first Albigensian crusade (1209-1213)

In the name of Pope Innocent III and with the full powers invested in him, the true spiritual and military leader of the crusade was Arnaud-Amaury, the Abbot of Cîteaux; he was given full powers to eradicate the heresy and benefited from the full support of Simon de Montfort.
With the authorisation of King Philip Augustus, but without his participation or his having appointed a representative, the vassals of the King of France took part in this crusade. Most of the army gathered in Lyons, travelled down the Rhone Valley and started its campaign in Valence.
The problem of funding was very different from other crusades. Philip Augustus did not want to make a contribution from royal funds, therefore, the Pope asked the French prelates to urge the population to make a voluntary contribution of one tenth of its income. Also, in order for the crusaders to be able to finance their journey and equipment (horses, weapons, etc.), the Pope asked the archbishops and the King to force the creditors of future crusades to defer demands for repayment and to provide an allowance on interest for the duration of the crusade.
Dictated by the rhythm of the seasons and the duration of the ost (40 days), the first crusade involved the following military operations:
- from 22 July to end of October 1209: from Béziers to Pamiers and Montréal;
- from March to November 1210: between Carcassonne and Castres;
- summer 1211: around Lavaur, siege of Toulouse and Cathar uprising near Castelnaudary;
- winter 1211: sieges and fighting around Albi;
- spring 1212: new campaign of sieges around Albi;
- summer and autumn 1212: gradual surrounding of Toulouse;
- January 1213: Innocent III decrees an immediate end to the crusade.

The keep at Beaucaire Castle (Gard).

The first campaign (summer-autumn 1209)

The aim of the crusade was to remove heresy by obtaining (still in the feudal framework) the submission of the lords who, by undertaking to promote this eradication, would save their fiefs which, in turn, would become untouchable. The protection of the Church was extended to all those who became active participants in the crusade. It was agreed to ride through all the fiefs.

The bulk of the army set out from Lyons, passed through Valence, which was the first town to submit, as was the nearest lord to this town. This army of several tens of thousands of people (fighters and those accompanying them) crossed the River Rhone at Beaucaire.

How did the Church justify the crusade against the Cathars?

For we 21st century people, it is difficult to understand how the papacy could organise and manage an armed intervention in a Christian country. However, this is less difficult to understand in the context of medieval mentalities for which religion was an integral part of all actions and thinking. Any form of deviation was seen as being outside the normal order.

When it came to heresy, and particularly the Cathar heresy, the Church initially adopted a strictly spiritual attitude; for example, the Councils of Reims (1049) and Toulouse (1058) recalled the weapons at the Church's disposal not to punish but to help sinners, heretics, to redeem themselves: excommunication, fasting, pilgrimage, or even a crusade in the Holy Land.

But, the spread of theocratic thinking led to the idea that, because the Pope was the supreme representative of God on earth, the position of a heretic was that of a rebellious subject. The Church's court (generally presided over the by the Bishop of the diocese in which the heretic lived) could hand down spiritual sentences, but it also had to act in the same way as a secular court, the purpose of which was to hand down material punishments (branding on the shoulder with a red-hot iron, confiscation of property, banishment, etc.). Therefore, the Church required a secular authority designed, firstly, to capture heretics and, secondly, to punish them..

Pope Innocent II burning heretics.
Manuscript from 1416.
Bibliothèque Nationale,
Paris, Ms 5077 RES, f° 360 v°.

Raymond Roger Trencavel (whose seal is visible) under the first attack of the crusaders' army in summer 1209, despite his having presented his surrender to the leaders of the crusade for the towns of Béziers, Carcassonne, Albi and Rayès. His situation quickly became critical in view of the intransigence of the papal legates. On 2 July 1209, Béziers became the first stage of the Cathar tragedy; about twenty thousand people were massacred by the crusaders and it was here that the terrible words were pronounced: "Kill them all, God will know his own".

Musée du Biterrois, Béziers.

The start of the crusade was relatively peaceful and everything went well in Valence. The same applied to Montpellier (a fief of the King of Aragon Peter II) which the Pope wished to safeguard. The army was about to enter the lands belonging to Trencavel, the Viscount of Béziers, Carcassonne, Albi and Rayès. Trencavel offered the legate (in fact there were three of these but the main one was Arnaud-Amaury) his submission, but this was refused because the papacy believed that the vassals, mostly acquired through the Cathar cause, would not acknowledge this submission (remember that this would make all the Viscount's lands untouchable).

The legate's refusal marked a turning point in events, with the Viscount calling upon his vassals to prepare an armed resistance.

Saint-Nazaire Cathedral in Béziers.

The crusaders reached Béziers on 21 July 1209 and the way in which the events unfolded was, in some respects, exemplary. Viscount Trencavel, for strategic reasons, abandoned Béziers accompanied by certain people (Jews and some Cathars) whom he believed to be particularly in danger, in order to gather his forces near Carcassonne.

An event of great significance followed. The Bishop (Catholic) of Béziers attempted to prevent the worst-case scenario, something which, by all accounts, he had foreseen, by requesting a meeting with the crusaders. These gave the following ultimatum: the Catholics of Béziers should hand over the heretics (a list of whom had been provided by the Bishop himself) or leave the town "in order to avoid sharing their fate and perishing with them". These threatening words begged one small question: which heretics were they referring to (Perfects, believers) and how many of them were there?

It is difficult to answer this question without being certain that we do actually have the right document. The list we do have gives the names of 223 people and was provided by the Bishop and it is likely that the people which appear on it were Perfects (because the figure is probably too low to be just believers).

Whatever the case, the population of Béziers (more likely its representatives in charge of municipal affairs) rejected this ultimatum. The bishop left the town with a few other Catholics to join the crusaders camp, but the priests (Catholic) remained in Béziers.

On 27 July, the town was attacked resulting in a bloodbath. There was pillaging and fires, but, above all, the entire population was massacred, including the priests (20,000 people is the figure given in the papal legates' report). This was the moment when the Abbot of Cîteaux pronounced the terrible words: "Kill them all, God will know his own".

Massacre of Béziers by Simon de Montfort's troops.
Wood engraving from 1875, from a drawing by Emile Bayard. AKG-Images.

The massacre of Béziers

Without carrying out a gruesome count that certainly would not lessen the horrific nature of this massacre, it is, nonetheless, necessary to be cautious when giving details about the number of victims. In general, accounts from that period always provide very exaggerated figures: one chronicler suggested that the crusaders' army comprised 500,000 men (namely at least ten times more than might feasibility be believed). In the case of the massacres and deaths by fire to which the Perfects, the believers and ordinary people were subjected, it should be recalled that the customs of that time were not gentle and that any harsh behaviour was reinforced by the fanaticism which spread very quickly.
The massacre of Béziers was significant in three respects: firstly, it came at the start of the crusade, therefore it served to create terror and a desire for vengeance; secondly, it was linked to the famous words – "Kill them all, God will know his own"; and, finally, it involved the entire population, probably about 20,000 people.

The terrible words: "Kill them all, God will know his own" (Béziers, July 1209)

In the collective memory, these words are often attributed to Simon de Montfort. In actual fact, they were spoken by a German Cistercian monk, Caesar of Heisterbach, who was not present at the events, who put them into the mouth of the papal legate, Arnaud-Amaury, Abbot of Cîteaux, appointed by Innocent III to lead the crusade (owing to the King of France's refusal to participate or to appoint a representative). Is this attribution correct?

It is true that, at the siege of Béziers, Simon de Montfort was still just a simple participant, without any specific responsibility, and there is nothing to support his being behind these words.

For Arnaud-Amaury, during another tragic affair, the death by fire in Minerve, he replied to a lord who was surprised at his – very relative – clemency towards the castle's inhabitants: "Do not fear, there will not be many" (to abjure, therefore, to save).

In all events, these words correspond to a very common state of mind among the crusaders which can be seen in various documents. There was a very clear intention to carry out a massacre. At the start of the siege, the Bishop had prompted Catholics to leave Béziers so as not to share the fate of the heretics and perish alongside them. Therefore, there clearly had been a threat of extermination.

Some authors have wanted to free the legates of their responsibility in this massacre by putting it down to what would now be referred to as a few "uncontrollable elements". However, the scale of what happened casts doubt on this argument. On the contrary, perhaps we should see it as a deliberate attempt to sow terror in other towns wishing to resist? It should also be pointed out that the Count of Toulouse, a member of the crusade, was a direct witness to the tragedy.

Pont Vieux and Béziers Cathedral.

Narbonne, Montpellier, Cavaillon and many other towns took their oath, with the following obligations, interesting to note in view of their severity:

— to help the crusaders materially and financially;

— to hand over heretics and suspects to the crusaders so that they could appear before a religious tribunal made up of the crusade's main prelates (archbishops and bishops).

Simon de Montfort
(born around 1165 – died in 1218)

He was the emblematic figure of the military crusade against the Cathars, even if he is wrongly attributed with the terrible words cited above. He was a pure product of the feudal system and came from a noble family from Montfort-l'Amaury, whose lands covered the area around Rambouillet (Vaux-de-Cernay) and the nearby region of Mantes (Epernon, Houdan). He was a descendant of the English royal family and, through one of his ancestors, had an indirect link to the French royal family of which he was a vassal.

During a meeting held in 1199 in Escry-sur-Aisne (near Rethel), the purpose of which was a tournament, he signed up for the fourth crusade (the one deviated from its religious purpose by the Venetians and which, among other things, led to the sacking of the Christian city of Constantinople by the crusaders in 1204). From the outset, he refused to participate in the expedition against Zara, which aimed to conquer the Venetians, and travelled direct to the Holy Land where he spent one year.

In 1207, his cousin Guy, the Abbot of Vaux-de-Cernay, was asked by the Pope to carry out a preaching mission against the heretics in Languedoc. When, in 1208, Pope Innocent III decided to initiate a crusade against the Cathars, Simon de Montfort signed up, after the King of France, Philip Augustus, authorised his vassals to participate in it, without himself agreeing to do so.

At the start of this crusade, he did not play a leading role, but after the taking of Carcassonne, he was appointed (no doubt on the initiative of his cousin, Abbot Guy) as the successor to Raymond-Roger Trencavel, Viscount of Béziers and Carcassonne, deprived of his title owing to the support he had lent to the Cathar cause. His history is associated with the bloody conquest of the lands of this Viscountcy. He was killed in June 1218 during the siege of Toulouse, having become a focus of hatred and vengeance as a result of the massacres he had organised.

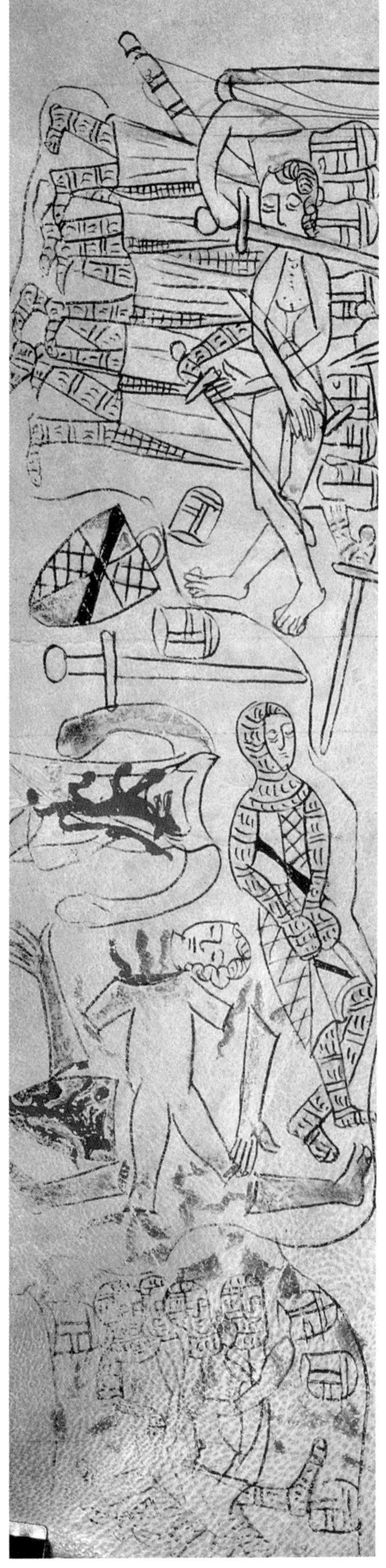

The death of Simon de Montfort.
Simon de Montfort died on 25 June 1218 during the siege of Toulouse.
Illumination from the first half of the 13th century.
London, British Library. AKG-Images/British Library.

Carcassonne at dusk.

The siege of Carcassonne started on 1 August 1209 with the arrival of a new player on the stage, the King of Aragon, who tried to set up mediation between his vassal, the Viscount of Béziers and Carcassonne, in charge of resistance operations, and the crusaders. The legates' ultimatum was very similar to the one for Béziers and came after the crusaders seized an important feature in the town's defence system. In actual fact, the crusaders, supported by the legates, feared that only the Viscount and eleven other men would leave the town abandoning it and its population to the mercy of the crusaders. However, Trencavel refused and decided to remain with the town's defenders.

Peter II, disapproving this ultimatum, left the region and returned to Aragon.

A few days later, Trencavel was taken prisoner in dubious circumstances: did he surrender or was he arrested after coming to negotiate? He died in captivity in November 1209. The town was taken on 15 August and the entire population was expelled and its property was confiscated.

The taking of Carcassonne marked the start of a new period in line with the spirit of crusades as imagined and defined by the Pope, but which was in complete contradiction to the feudal system. Remember that, at that time, the Viscount, the fief's leader, was still alive. However, the legate, acting in the name of the Pope, declared the Viscount to be dispossessed and announced that the fief was going to be allocated to a new lord: an acknowledgement of the existence of the suzerain Peter II of Aragon.

To whom could this fief be attributed? Arnaud-Amaury asked three lords (the Duke of Burgundy, the Count of Nevers, the Count of Saint-Pol) in turn to take over this fief but they declined. In actual fact, this method of transferring fiefs would not have been approved by the King of France, who, as the direct suzerain of these three lords, should have been consulted.

An alternative solution was found: offering the fief to a much more modest lord who did not have any direct vassality links with the King of France. Simon de Montfort was chosen. In this way, the person whose name was forever to be linked to the crusade against the Albigensians entered on to the stage of history. A small lord with minor fiefs, Simon de Montfort gave his agreement at a time when some of the crusaders, at the end of their ost, started to return to "France". A change was made to the way in which the crusade was to be organised. Now, although Arnaud-Amaury continued to be the main leader, the crusade now had a true warrior in charge of military operations.

In all events, the forces at Simon de Montfort's disposal were greatly reduced. All that remained after the forty days of ost were knights from the gentry of Ile-de-France with reinforcements not being available until the following spring (with the next ost).

But the crusade itself took on a new turn, no doubt the original goal, with the continued extermination of heretics, but also another aspect, the setting up of a new lord in the seat of the Viscountcy of Béziers and Carcassonne. The feudal system required that this person receive the homage of his vassals, meaning that he had to be recognised by them as the suzerain. The mechanisms of the feudal system came into play and although some vassals fully recognised their new suzerain, others refused to do so, resulting in an armed intervention aimed either at forcing them to take the oath of fealty and homage, or at expelling them (which gave Simon de Montfort the opportunity to "reward" some of his loyal servants by granting them a lord's land).

This overlapping of two objectives is one of the keys to understanding this new period in the history of the crusade designed to establish the new suzerain's authority over the areas he had received as fiefs.

Carcassonne.
Clever lighting reveals the ramparts and Carcassonne castle. Here the Porte d'Aude gate.

Inhabitants of Toulouse burning heretics.
Manuscript from 1296, extract from *Trésor des Histoires*, illumination by Maître de Boucicaut. Bibliothèque Nationale, Paris, Ms lat. 9187, f° 31 v°.

To this is added a financial aspect; Simon de Montfort, wishing to win favour with the papacy and also, in some respects, in order to thank the legates, decided to collect a tax in his new Viscountcy for the benefit of Rome following an idea clearly based on theocracy. He spoke of the "Roman Church's right of ownership". This again was a violation of feudal law since it spurned the existence of the suzerain, the King of Aragon. It is true that, unlike the King of France, the King of Aragon too was a vassal of the Pope.

Therefore, Simon de Montfort undertook a series of forays: to Limoux (southwest of Carcassonne) and to Castres (southwest). Here, an event occurred that was going to become very common: the execution of Cathars by fire. Two people were burnt at the stake, in violation of the rules laid out by the papacy which stated that those found guilty of heresy by the ecclesiastical court, presided over by the local bishop or his representative, should be handed over to the "secular arm" (namely the civil authorities) which would judge them and hand down the sentence.

Simon de Montfort chose to ignore these instructions since he was the sole person to judge, sentence and carry out the sentence: the road to death by fire was open.

Entrance to Minerve Castle.

Death by fire

The policy of death by fire in the crusade against the Albigensians is a result of the outbreak of brute force and the evolution of the concept of heresy. Pope Innocent III had acted to ensure that heresy was seen as an offence, punishable as such by secular power, and even a crime of lese-majesty which meant a person's tongue being torn out or death by fire.

The very first death by fire was not carried out during the repression of the Cathar heresy, but the punishment was very common and, in the collective memory, has become the symbol of the violence of the "French" troops and the Church. This involved burning alive

Minerve.
It was in Minerve (between Béziers and Carcassonne) that Simon de Montfort carried out the very first deaths by fire (about 140 victims) in July 121

(without any preliminaries such as strangling) those who refused to renounce the Cathar faith, or who had relapsed, meaning those who, after renouncing the Cathar faith, had returned to it.
Death by fire concerned mainly Perfects, but sometimes was also a sentence handed down to simple believers.
The main events where this method was used were at Minerve Castle (140 people in 1210), Lavaur Castle (400 people in 1211), Cassès (600 people in 1211), Montségur (200 people in 1244) and Agen (80 people in 1249).

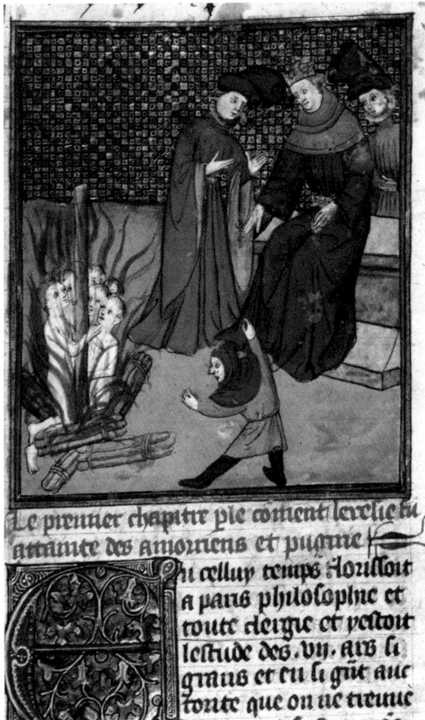

Amalrician heretics burnt before Philip II Augustus. This scene shows what death by fire for Cathars may have involved.
Extract from Les Grandes Chroniques de France, manuscript from the end of the 14th century. Bibliothèque Municipale de Lyon, Ms P. A 30.

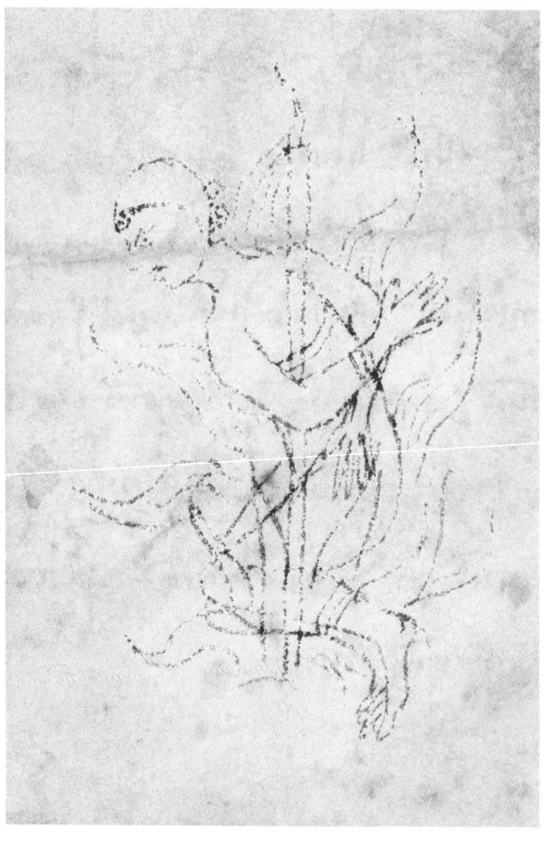

A heretic at the stake. This depiction of a heretic at the stake is very significant of a certain state of mind because, interestingly, it appears at the bottom of a proposed papal bull requested (in around 1250) by Alphonse of Poitiers, Saint Louis's brother, who led the final campaign against the heretics.
Archives Nationales, Paris.

On their way home, at the end of August, the crusaders experienced their first defeat when they attempted to take the Castle of Cabaret, whose lord, very close to the Cathars (no doubt he himself was one) and a loyal vassal of Trencavel, refused to surrender to Simon de Montfort.

Returning in their footsteps southwards via Fanjeaux, the crusaders veered westwards to take Pamiers. This was yet another violation of feudal law. This town was covered by a combined vassalage, or rather a shared vassalage, because the suzerain was the Abbey of Saint-Antonin and the Count of Foix; the abbot asked Simon de Montfort to replace the Count of Foix, which he did in September 1209.

A return northwards with the homage of Lombers and Albi (where the lord was the bishop), and, at the end of September, the Count of Foix, rightly annoyed by what had happened in Pamiers, attacked but was stopped quickly in Fanjeaux.

In autumn 1209, the situation became difficult for Simon de Montfort. The King of Aragon refused to recognise him as his vassal. The death of Trencavel in November at the age of 24 years (probably murdered in prison) did not help matters. Under conditions which can only be imagined, his widow signed an agreement with Simon de Montfort whereby she renounced her rights and those of her son (aged 2 years) in return for a yearly allowance. However, above all, the minor lords who had made their oath to Simon de Montfort (either the Occitan lords who had taken the oath, or the French lords who had replaced the Occitan lords who had been killed or who had fled) rebelled and these uprisings constantly needed to be quashed.

Simon de Montfort's annual campaigns (1210, 1211, 1212)

Every year, the process was the same: the arrival of new crusaders (lured by the seigniories to be conquered or acquired), forays to take rebel castles where Perfects were hiding, and their execution by fire, the setting up of new lords, the return home of the crusaders after the ost, uprisings in new areas in the autumn, etc.

These campaigns were characterised by exceptionally cruel events, for example, the torture of the inhabitants of Bram. In view of the religious fanaticism of the legates, some of the Catholic clergy and the crusaders, and their limited numbers (for example, in September 1209, at the end of the ost, Simon de Montfort had just twenty-six knights, although these were accompanied by their soldiers), the main, and, sometimes, the sole objective of the crusaders was to generate fear and to spread terror in order to maintain control over the situation.

The torture of the defenders of Bram

Bram is a village situated northwest of Carcassonne, which at the time of the Cathars, had no natural defences because it was built on the plain and, therefore, it was easy to attack. Among the prisoners taken, Simon de Montfort found a French priest (that is not Occitan) to whom he had entrusted the mission of guarding the town of Montréal after it had been abandoned by its Occitan lord (who refused to take an oath). However, this monk chose to return the town to its lord. The Bishop of Carcassonne stripped him of his ecclesiastical position and Simon de Montfort then tied him to a horse and dragged him through the town before having him hanged.

However, above all, Simon de Montfort had the eyes gouged out and the noses cut off of about a hundred prisoners and sent them to Cabaret guided by a prisoner who had had one eye spared.

Puivert Castle, situated southwest of Carcassonne.
It was laid siege to and was defeated by the crusaders in 1210.

The vaulted room known as the Musicians' Hall in Puivert Castle.

Recounting these expeditions in detail would be fastidious, therefore, we will simply provide details of just a few of them, highlighting the fact that this military activity was mainly in the region of Carcassonne and, moving northwards, approached Toulouse.

1210

MARCH

— with the arrival of a contingent of crusaders led by his wife Alix, Simon de Montfort attacked the village of Montlaur (northeast of Carcassonne), which had revolted against the French garrison, and hanged all the inhabitants who had not managed to flee;

— attack on the village of Bram (west of Carcassonne) and torture of the prisoners.

APRIL

— attack on the village of Cabaret (north of Carcassonne); siege and taking of Alaric Castle (southeast of Carcassonne).

JULY

— siege and taking of Minerve Castle (northeast of Carcassonne); death by fire for 140 Cathars.

AUGUST-NOVEMBER

— siege and taking of the Castles of Termes (southeast of Carcassonne) and Puivert (southwest).

1211

MARCH

— new forays with the arrival of new crusaders. Capitulation of Cabaret Castle.

MAY

— siege and taking of Lavaur Castle (between Albi and Toulouse). Death by fire for 300 to 400 Cathars, the highest number in the entire Cathar tragedy. Taking of Les Cassès (southwest of Castelnaudary); death by fire for about 60 Cathars.

JUNE

— failure of the siege of Toulouse.

1212

WINTER AND SPRING

— the crusaders' forays start again to win back the castles and towns which had been retaken by the enemy, especially in the Lauragais area; this was possible thanks to the return to Europe of crusaders from the Holy Land, led by Guy, Simon de Montfort's brother.

SUMMER

— conquest of lower Quercy and the region of Agen (siege of Saint-Antonin, Penne-d'Agenais, Moissac).

During these years, what was happening with the Count of Toulouse? To answer this question, we will have to go back a few years.

The Count of Toulouse and the crusade

All historians have questioned his character and the political and religious intentions behind his equivocation because it is difficult to understand what guided his behaviour.

Earlier, we saw that, at the start of the crusade, Raymond VI asked the legates for help and swore peace with them. This oath was taken in Saint-Gilles in June 1209. But, although he undertook to participate in the crusade, he still had to have the excommunication placed on him in 1207 withdrawn, as well as the accusation of having murdered Pierre de Castelnau. However, his commitment to the crusade placed his lands under the protection of the Pope. He spent the forty days of ost, which he owed under feudal law, as discreetly as possible because he did not want to act against his vassals. We do not have any documents attesting to his behaviour during the pillage and massacre of Béziers.

The legates and Simon de Montfort did not believe in Raymond VI's oath to participate in the crusade, and, to contribute to the fight against the Cathars. Therefore, in the second half of 1209, Simon de Montfort asked him to hand over the Cathars in Toulouse. The Count refused to do so and, once again, he was excommunicated and the accusations made against him (barely three months earlier!), which had been withdrawn at the ceremony of penitence in Saint-Gilles, were applied again.

But, this time, the Count of Toulouse called upon the help of the Pope (and even travelled to Rome at the end of 1209). He managed to obtain a form of reprieve because it was decided that the legates should assemble a council by May 1210 which would receive the Count's "canonic purgation", meaning that it would hear his defence (because remember that the sentences of excommunication and interdict had been handed down without the accused being heard!) and either absolve him or transmit a request for his punishment to the Pope.

View over Lauragais plain, between Toulouse and the Montagne Noire.

The taking of Minerve (July 1210)

Minerve was the site of the first death by burning organised by Simon de Montfort on 22 July 1210. The siege started on about 15 June and lasted for five weeks under conditions made even more difficult by the heat and the lack of water for those under siege. According to the terms of the capitulation decided by Simon de Montfort and the legate Arnaud-Amaury, all the people in the castle and the village would be saved if they gave their oath of loyalty to the Catholic Church. Among the inhabitants were some Perfects and Cathar followers from both sexes who refused to abjure. A fire was prepared below the castle on around 22 July and the Cathars threw themselves on to it voluntarily: about 140 men and women.

Lord William of Minerve was dispossessed of his land which was given to Simon de Montfort.

Minerve.
This was the site of the first death by fire organised by Simon de Montfort after a siege lasting five weeks.

In July 1210, this council met in Saint-Gilles once again, but this time in the presence of the Count. However, the legate Arnaud-Amaury, who was very hostile to him, succeeded in avoiding the main debate (was the Count a heretic? was he an accomplice in Pierre de Castelnau's assassination?) by arguing that the accused had not answered the other questions raised in 1209, for example those concerning the collection of illegal tolls and the construction of fortresses on land belonging to the Church, etc. The Council decided to renew his excommunication dating from 1209 (the third time in three years).

The situation on the ground became complicated with a growing number of lords who had refused to take an oath to Simon de Montfort and who had had their land confiscated, taking refuge in areas belonging to the Count of Toulouse. We saw earlier that the crusaders did not hesitate in June 1211 to lay siege to Toulouse, although they failed to win it, and that 1212 was devoted to quelling revolts and re-establishing vassals loyal to Simon de Montfort, which could only mean a hardening of the Count of Toulouse's attitude, who found himself bombarded with complaints from his vassals.

In January 1211, a new summit meeting was organised (firstly in Narbonne then in

Saint-Gilles: spiral staircase and the remains of the church's Romanesque choir.

Montpellier), but this time its purpose was truly political and brought together the legates and the four major lords from the region: Simon de Montfort, the King of Aragon, the Count of Toulouse and the Count of Foix. The legates obtained a victory at just the right time: Peter II of Aragon, retracting his previous position, agreed to receive homage from Simon de Montfort for the fief over which he had become lord (Béziers and Carcassonne), therefore, agreeing to recognise him as a legitimate vassal. Wishing to continue with their progress, the legates asked the Count of Toulouse to become involved in the fight against the Cathars in exchange for maintaining his rights over his own property and over the heretic villages in his fiefs (which would prevent Simon de Montfort from establishing lords indebted to him). Raymond VI refused. The legates decided to go even further and presented him with some new demands, especially the demolition of fortresses (with the Count having to travel to the Holy Land and remain there until the legates authorised him to return) although the requirement for him to participate in the fight against the Cathars was withdrawn. These requests were so unusual that historians generally believe they were a provocation and it is easy to understand why Raymond VI chose not to reply and to return immediately to Toulouse.

In February 1212, the legates decreed a new excommunication (the fourth) and placed an interdict on the entire county (a decision by the Pope) exposing the Count's lands to attack, meaning that since he was dispossessed of his titles and feudal rights, the crusaders could take control of them.

The war against the Count of Toulouse and his supporters was open.

Castelnaudary.
In around 1210, Simon de Montfort led a battle here which proved to be indecisive. 1211 and 1212 were marked mainly by the conflict between Simon de Montfort and the Count of Toulouse.

Undoubtedly, some of the population of Toulouse openly supported the heretics hounded by the crusaders. The Bishop of Toulouse Fulk, appointed by the Pope, had sought to divert this support by creating a "white brotherhood" comprising those who supported the fight against the heretics, with the use of force if necessary. In reaction to this measure, an incitement to civil war, the Cathar supporters created a "black brotherhood".

Another element can be seen in this wish by the legates and Simon de Montfort to bring the Count of Toulouse to heel which had nothing whatsoever to do with the religious question. This was Simon de Montfort's desire to replace Raymond VI at the head of this prestigious county as he had succeeded in doing for the Viscountcy of Béziers and Carcassonne.

No decisive events occurred in 1211 and 1212 in the direct conflict with Toulouse with the failure of the siege of the city and the indecisive outcome of the Battle of Castelnaudary. Simon de Montfort slowly encouraged those serving him to deprive the Count of Toulouse of the support of his vassals or neighbours, because, naturally, the complex network of feudal links between Raymond VI and his vassals had its weaknesses which simply needed to be undermined. This was the case of Quercy, whose lords lent their support to Simon de Montfort in June 1211.

In October 1212, Simon de Montfort and his lieutenants (especially his brother Guy) succeeded in politically isolating Toulouse and, at the end of 1212; it became obvious that political concerns had taken precedence over religious concerns. Simon de Montfort had managed to strengthen his position as lord and had obtained the trust of the legates because he had succeeded in having himself recognised, receiving homage (or having men loyal to him placed at the head of his fiefs) for a very large number of territories: Viscountcy of Béziers and Carcassonne, County of Toulouse, County of Comminges. Of course, there remained the problem of Toulouse itself and the attitude of the King of Aragon (who had always refused to pay homage to this new Viscount of Béziers and Carcassonne, refusing to recognise him despite the undertaking made in 1211).

> Saint-Nazaire cathedral in Béziers seen from Pont Vieux.

Lagrasse Abbey in Aude.

> The living quarters at Lagrasse Abbey (Aude).

It was at this moment (November 1212) that a very significant political event took place which showed the extent to which this crusade against the Albigensians had become a venture to replace the Occitan, southern feudal system with the "French" northern system. Simon de Montfort convened an assembly in Pamiers to prepare a text called the "Statute of Pamier". This was an attempt to define "customs", namely the rules of legal life. In short, the aim was to introduce the rules used in Ile-de-France, something that was stated clearly in the agreement signed between Simon de Montfort and his vassals. This text was not part of the Statute (which contained 46 articles), which, in itself, was a major innovation:

"Customs which the Lord Count should observe between himself and the Barons of France and others to whom he has given land in this country:

As much between Barons and Knights as between bourgeois and peasants, successions will be based on the custom of usage in France around the city of Paris.

No Baron, Knight or any other Lord in our land will agree to a duel in his court of justice for whatever reason with the exception of treason, theft, pillage or murder.

In courts, legal affairs, dowries, fiefs and sharing of land, the Count must guarantee the Barons of France and others to whom he has given land in this country, the same usages and customs as those observed in France around the city of Paris.

Signed in Pamiers at our Palace on 1 December in the year 1212 of the Incarnation of the Lord."

The intervention of the King of Aragon

Aware of the threat weighing on him, Raymond VI undertook a manoeuvre which highlights the complex nature of the Cathar affair. By travelling to Aragon, he was going to ask assistance from King Peter II, whose "orthodox" religious beliefs could not be doubted. The King had led and continued to lead an armed fight against the Muslims who were occupying Spain, meaning that he was leading a "true" crusade in the traditional sense of the word (and had just been victorious at Las Navas). However, the King of Aragon could not accept that a lord from the North, from France, could gradually acquire a huge area of land which might not only be an obstacle to his own ambitions, but also, pose a threat to him in the short term. Also, the family factor must have played a role since the two lords were brothers-in-law (Peter II's sister was Raymond VI's wife).

The conflict was about to become a fight between two cultures: Occitan and French. The intervention of the King of Aragon was going to be the last chance to save Toulouse, as Raymond VI explained to Peter II at the end of September 1212, and he obtained his support very easily.

A particularly interesting point is the fact that Peter II wanted to justify his intervention in canonic terms and prepared a very watertight argument:

— the Pope had defined clearly the objectives of the crusade: to depose those who protect heretics, to confiscate their property and to transfer it to good Catholics;

Interdict.
Interdict was one of the sanctions handed down by the Church to heretics. This involved forbidding any form of religious life inside a territory. Only christenings were allowed.
Painting by Jean-Paul Laurens, 1875. Le Havre, Musée des Beaux-Arts André Malraux.

— in actual fact, the confiscations and transfers had involved estates whose lords were neither heretics nor accomplices (for example on the land of direct vassals of the King of Aragon). The fact of having asked lords to take an oath, without having tried them for heresy, meant that they were considered to be good Catholics, therefore, having confiscated their land because they did not want to take the oath did not have anything to do with the religious problem. Also, the duty of fealty to a lord implied the suzerain's agreement, a feudal principle violated by the crusaders in the fiefs belonging to the Count of Foix, the Count of Comminges and even in the region of Agen (because these belonged to the Count of Toulouse who had acquired them from Richard Lionheart by marrying his sister Joan in 1196).

All these arguments were presented to Innocent III by a delegation from Aragon which travelled to Rome in November 1212. The result was positive. The Pope decreed an immediate end to the crusade, the restitution to Peter II and his vassals of all their rights and agreed to Peter II's proposal to draw up a definitive agreement.

At this stage in the events, it is important to study the timescale. In November 1212 the delegation from Aragon travelled to Rome and in the middle of January 1213, the Pope informed the legates of his decision to put a stop to the crusade. However, it took one month (February 1213) for this information to reach the legates during which time the situation had changed completely.

Remember that the Pope had enjoined the legates (end 1209-start 1210) to proceed with the canonic trial which would allow Raymond VI to finally explain himself over the accusation of heresy. The legates had prevaricated and, in actual fact, they had skirted the papal instructions. Innocent III repeated these instructions and the legates were forced to prepare this trial, the reason for a meeting of prelates involved in the crusade held in Lavaur at the start of January 1213 (therefore, in complete ignorance of the Pope's decision to stop the crusade). Peter II of Aragon travelled to this council but the discussions started on a wrong foot because of a misunderstanding: Arnaud-Amaury only wanted to deal with questions of procedure concerning the trial, while the King of Aragon repeated the theories presented to the Pope by his delegation with a view to ending the conflict, namely returning land and rights to his vassals and Raymond VI's penitence with the transfer of his succession to his son. The legates rejected these proposals and, above all, the position of arbitrator adopted, in some respects, by the King. On 27 January, the Count of Toulouse, his son, the vassals of the King and the Consuls of Toulouse, made an oath to Peter II and accepted in advance the decisions he would take to resolve the conflict with the crusaders. In order to fully understand the scope of such an act, it is necessary to understand what it meant in feudal law. The signatories placed themselves under the protection of the King of Aragon, with the ambivalence we have already spoken of several times (the duties of the one "receiving" and those of the one who "offers himself" being part of a whole). Yet, the Count of Toulouse was a vassal of the King of France and, consequently, he could not "give himself" to another suzerain.

All this relied heavily on the proposals which, according to the Pope, Peter II should make at a later date. In short, the King of Aragon was gradually developing his own interests without taking account of the spirit and the content of the papal decision.

Do we really need to underline the fact that the legates judged Peter II's attitude very severely and decided to share their feelings with the Pope (the bull cancelling the crusade had not yet reached them!)? On 21 May 1213, the Pope decided to relaunch the crusade which he had stopped on 15 January and ordered Peter II to declare void the oaths taken in Toulouse on 27 January and to sign a truce with Simon de Montfort, failing which he would be excluded from the Catholic community.

The crusaders' forays had continued throughout this period as well as the reposts of the Occitan knights which led to the devastation of the countryside around Toulouse and the taking and taking back of castles, etc. Peter II decided to organise a proper military campaign and crossed the Pyrenees with an army, the size of which is not known but, most certainly, was large.

This army marched to Toulouse with a view to taking Muret. However, it encountered an army of crusaders which had just departed from Fanjeaux.

The Battle of Muret proved to be decisive. The death of Peter II, military defeat and the crushing of the Aragon and Toulouse armies opened wide the way for Simon de Montfort's unlimited domination over the region. It is easy to understand why his name is still very much alive in Occitan collective memory.

Padern Castle.
It is situated between those of Quéribus and Aguilar, lying between Perpignan and Narbonne. It was occupied by the crusaders. The lord of the castle was a supporter of the Count of Toulouse and helped to defend Toulouse in 1219.

Battle of Muret (1213). Simon de Montfort defeated Raymond of Toulouse and Peter II of Aragon, and led the defeated Albigensians naked into captivity.
Extract from *Chroniques de Saint-Denis*. Manuscript from 1350. London, British Library. AKG-Images/British Library.

The Battle of Muret (12 September 1213)

Muret is situated south of Toulouse. Peter II on his way to meet Simon de Montfort's troops, decided to seize this town defended by a small number of crusaders along the way. The siege started on 30 August 1213, shortly before Simon de Montfort himself arrived near Muret.

Peter II's followers set up a camp three kilometres from Muret, on the hills overlooking the plain. The Count of Toulouse and the King of Aragon disagreed on which tactic to adopt, with the first proposing to wait until the camp was attacked, and the latter wanting to leave the camp and attack the town, thus taking advantage of their greater numbers (2,000 mounted soldiers compared to 900 crusaders).

Peter II was killed at the start of the fighting which spread panic through the Aragon camp, and the crusaders' cavalry (mainly French) chose that moment to attack the enemy infantry on its way to Muret forcing it back to the Garonne River. Half of the foot soldiers (about 15,000 to 20,000 men out of 40,000) perished, either slaughtered or drowned.

The completion of the conquest (1214-1215)

Deprived of all major support after the death of the King of Aragon, Raymond VI found himself powerless to deal with Simon de Montfort's rise in power.

The latter initially set out towards the region of Foix, then travelled to Provence via lower Languedoc and the Rhone valley. The reason for these forays was that, despite the outcome of the Battle of Muret, the lords and local populations were still not prepared to surrender and they had started to revolt. Therefore, matters were not really resolved and a new Aragon army even established itself close to Narbonne. It was driven back, but a new obstacle, this time a political one, lay in the path of the domination of Languedoc: the Pope.

In January 1214, Innocent III appointed a new legate, Pierre de Bénevent, to replace Arnaud-Amaury, whose behaviour over the years had deviated greatly from the papal instructions. The new legate was given full powers and was required to apply the principles which Innocent III had decreed in 1209: no harm should be done to those who, by making an oath of peace, rejected the heretic cause and, thus, were placed under the protection of the papacy. It was clear that these principles were not in line with the ambitions of Simon de Montfort.

Foix Castle.
The lord of Foix Castle, as well as the local population refused to surrender for many years.

The situation became difficult for him again. Raymond VI laid siege to Moissac, held by the crusaders. The King of England, John Lackland, made his way to the region of Agen (lands which the Count of Toulouse had obtained from him as we saw earlier) and received the homage of the lords who had been forced to make an oath to the leader of the crusade.

The new legate tried to implement the Pope's instructions and succeeded in doing so better than his predecessors had done, obtaining the oath of peace of Narbonne, the Counts of Comminges and Foix, without any military intervention (April 1214). No crusaders were present at the oath of Narbonne.

Text of the submission of Raymond VI, Count of Toulouse, handed to the Pope's legate in April 1214

"I, Raymond, by the grace of God, Duke of Narbonne, Count of Toulouse, Marquis of Provence, give myself to Our Lord and the Holy Roman Church, and to you Lord Peter, Cardinal-Deacon, legate of the Holy See. I offer up to you my person with the intention of carrying out and observing faithfully, with all my power, all the orders regardless of what they are, which the Lord Pope and the mercy of your Holiness will consider right to accord to me. I will work effectively so that my son, with the land that he owns and possesses, places himself in your hands and offers up his person and his estates to you, or everything from his estates that pleases you, in order that he follows faithfully, according to his power, the orders of the Lord Pope and your own. Signed in Narbonne in the month of April, Wednesday, the year 1214 of the Incarnation of the Lord."
Text cited by M. Roquebert, *L'Epopée Cathare*, tome III, p. 262-263.

He also obtained the surrender of the city of Toulouse, which dissociated itself completely from the Count of Toulouse and his son, as well as the submission of Raymond VI himself. This was obtained without public humiliation. Clearly, Pierre de Bénevent was looking for efficiency rather than vengeance, a point which differentiated him notably from Arnaud-Amaury. Simon de Montfort's policy continued to be that of force and reinforcements were at his disposal because, with the fine weather, new contingents were gathering and heading towards the region between Béziers and Pézenas. Simon de Montfort took advantage of these to conquer Quercy, Agenais, Périgord, Rouergue (continuing with his "exploits", with events such as death by fire for seven heretics in Morlhon, south of Albi). This foray of destruction and massacres took place between May and the end of November 1214 and in doing so, once again, Simon de Montfort violated the framework defined by the Pope, for example, he usurped the role of the suzerain in Rouergue.

Heretics (Knights Templar) are burned at the stake. This scene gives an idea of what death by fire for Cathars might have involved.
Extract from *De la Création du Monde jusqu'à 1384*. AKG-Images/Erich Lessing.

An episode very revealing of the feelings inspired by the military leader of the crusade occurred at this moment. A council met in Montpellier in January 1215 to try to resolve the problems of peace and of faith by reaching an agreement between the prelates and the lords taking account of the oaths obtained by the legate. It was a vast undertaking, especially since the position of the crusaders (who were used to seizing seigniories in the name of the fight against heresy) and that of the Pope appeared to be in contradiction. However, the town of Montpellier, which had obtained political autonomy owing to the misfortune suffered by its theoretical suzerain, the King of Aragon, firmly opposed Simon de Montfort's entry within its walls, giving rise to a rather strange situation whereby the all-powerful military leader did not participate directly in the council and camped outside the town, meeting with the prelates when they themselves were not in meetings.

A new complication in the unfolding of these complex events which are sometimes difficult to understand: the Council decided unanimously that Simon de Montfort should become the supreme leader of Toulouse and the estates of the Count of Toulouse and the lands conquered by the crusaders! This would make him a lord more powerful than the King of France with control over an area of land stretching from the central Pyrenees to the Alps and up to the Dordogne. This proposal ignored both the intentions of the Pope and the rules of feudal law, because the rights of the supreme suzerains were quite simply forgotten (Kings of France, England, Aragon and even the Emperor).

Faced with such an outrage, which only mirrored Simon de Montfort's inordinate ambition, Pierre de Bénevent reacted firmly with a refusal in the name of the powers invested in him by the Pope: to obtain the oath of peace from heretics but not to make the seigniories subservient to Simon de Montfort.

Peyrepertuse Castle, the largest Cathar castle.

The Council called upon the Pope to reply positively in contradiction to the legate. In the meantime, Innocent III had received Raymond VI and had absolved him in exchange for him handing over his land and his rights to the Pope. This explains the delaying tactic used by the Pope, who submitted the decision to the Grand Council to be held in Lateran in 1215. Up until this Council, Simon de Montfort was going to continue with his same policy of force, clearly wanting to present the Pope with an irreversible fait accompli. In particular, he was going to use the moral support and authority of a player in the Cathar affair who had not yet appeared directly on the stage, but who was going to do so with the ulterior motive of increasing the power of his kingdom: the King of France.

Philip Augustus had always refused to intervene directly and, in particular, to take part in the crusade. When faced with Innocent III's many insistent requests, he had always laid out the argument of external difficulties: dispute with the King of England, dispute with one of the pretenders to the imperial German crown. But, in July 1214, all obstacles were removed with the victory at the Battle of Bouvines. However, the papacy's hold over the Albigensian area worried Philip Augustus, as it did the other Kings of France, who could not allow theocracy.

The King of France's entry on to the stage was going to take place in two acts, both very significant. Firstly, during the Council, Philip Augustus granted his protection to the town of Montpellier, which was a clever and effective method of marking his territory. Secondly, he authorised his son Louis (the future Louis VIII) to take part in the crusade for forty days (ost). As we will see, his arrival in the debate greatly favoured the political views of Philip Augustus, especially since Simon de Montfort was not fully trusted by the Pope and there were a growing number of disagreements between the military leader and the former religious leader, namely Arnaud-Amaury, who had proclaimed himself Duke and Archbishop of Narbonne. However, the entry into Toulouse of Simon de Montfort, Louis and the legate appeared to support the military leader.

The Council of the Lateran (1215)

By calling a particularly large council, Innocent III was not only hoping to resolve the Cathar problem once and for all, or more exactly the political problems resulting from the use of a military solution to solve a religious problem. His aim was much more general because he wanted to re-establish the authority of the Church, meaning with a clergy following a strict way of life and close to their flock, Therefore, the Council studied ecclesiastical discipline as well as dogma (particularly that of the Trinity) and religious policy (the obligation for every believer to confess at least once a year dates from the Council).

Fourth Council of the Lateran in Rome (1215). Pope Innocent III imposes discriminatory measures against heretics and introduces the Church's tax to prepare the fifth crusade.

19th century wood engraving. AKG-Images/Ullstein bild.

The Fourth Council of the Lateran

This Council, the fourth in name, met in 1215. It was an extremely important meeting through the decisions that were taken. 71 archbishops, 410 bishops, 800 abbots, and patriarchs from Jerusalem and Constantinople took part in it, as well as many representatives of Kings and major towns.

In the spirit of Innocent III, the initial aim of the council was to relaunch the crusade in the Holy Land (which had failed in 1212) and to implement far-reaching internal reforms. These involved examining a series of political problems concerning the Church's relationships and its interventions in the German Empire, in France and in England, as well as in Occitania, since the so-called Albigensian crusade had started in 1209.

It was this council which decreed the obligation for all Christians to confess at least once a year, and the obligation for Jews to wear different clothes from those of Christians.

The question of the Cathar heresy was addressed through the request made to the Pope by the Count of Toulouse to obtain the withdrawal of the sentence levelled against him. The sentence was confirmed with the transfer of his property to Simon de Montfort, the pursuit of the principle to expropriate the accomplices of heretics and the exile of the Count of Toulouse.

It should be noted that the council did not condemn (or make any allusion to the massacres already perpetrated) the methods employed by the crusaders to encourage the Occitan population to return to the Christian faith.

However, in terms of the Cathar affair, one absence and one decision should be remembered from this Council: the absence of any criticism of the barbaric methods used by the crusaders with no regret being expressed. This is not surprising when considering that, at that time, the Pope's voice could not take precedence over an entire Council and the majority of the participants largely supported Simon de Montfort and approved of his methods.

It was this same majority that imposed its views on the Pope and transferred the title of Count of Toulouse from Raymond VI, deprived of his rights, to Simon de Montfort. Only a few estates were sequestrated by the Pope, such as the Venaissin, to be handed over to Raymond VI's son at a later date. The rest was given to Simon de Montfort, subject to (in feudal law) his being invested of his rights by Philip Augustus, the supreme suzerain.

This formality was completed in April 1216 in Pont-de-l'Arche (Eure). Simon de Montfort had succeeded, but the King of France had also succeeded in placing himself at the forefront of the territorial governance for the Albigensian affair. On a regional level and on a religious and political level, nothing had been resolved. The Cathar church survived and the population's desire for independence was going to make itself felt.

Quéribus Castle, a safe and inviolate refuge for Cathars.

This "siege stone" sealed into the western wall of Saint-Nazaire cathedral in Carcassonne has been the subject of several hypotheses.
It may represent the siege of Toulouse and the death of Simon de Montfort.
AKG-Images/Erich Lessing.

The revolt: successes and setbacks (1216-1225)

It might have been believed that the almost complete removal of Raymond VI and the establishment of Simon de Montfort on a solid legal basis would lead to a period of peace, even though the situation had been imposed and was not approved by all.

The successes and victory of the Count of Toulouse

It was from Avignon that a huge movement of revolt was going to spread. In May 1216, the town of Avignon, in the presence of Raymond VI and his son, declared itself in favour of a military campaign to win back Toulouse and restore the "legitimate heir". As many texts testify, this movement could be said to have had a "national" undertone in that it expressed a very strong idea of a community of language, spirit and culture which could not accept the way in which the papacy, the Church and the "French" had dealt with the Cathar problem.

The number of people supporting them grew very quickly and included the Lord of Orange, the Count of Valentinois and the majority of the towns along the Rhone valley. Among these rebels were many defeated by the crusade, as well as others who had been uncertain or even supportive of the Church.

The first aim of this Occitan army was to take Beaucaire (where the son of the Count of Toulouse, Raymond the Younger, had been born), a town held by the crusaders. The Occitans surrounded the castle and fortified the town leaving the crusaders unable to free the castle or win back the town (August 1216).

At the same time, the city of Toulouse revolted and was sacked by Simon de Montfort in September 1216, but this did not prevent Raymond VI's victorious return to his capital one year later. In the meantime, the wind of revolt continued to spread to Carcassonne, the Corbières, Provence and the Rhone valley and, between June and September 1217, with the arrival of the crusaders, as in every year, for the forty day ost, Simon de Montfort made his way up the Rhone River as far as Montélimar and beyond.

The retaking of Toulouse by Raymond VI was a serious setback for Simon de Montfort and he decided to lay siege to the town in order to win it back. For the first time, the Occitan and the "French" came into direct contact in the presence of their leaders.

The siege lasted from October 1217 to June 1218. On 25 June, Simon de Montfort died, killed after being struck on the head by a stone during fighting. The legate appointed his son, Amaury, as his successor, but the impetus of the crusaders had been crushed with the loss of the hugely charismatic figure of Simon de Montfort and the siege was lifted at the end of July.

The crusaders' failure gave strength to the Occitan's desire to resist and, with the arrival of autumn Amaury de Montfort was going to find himself faced with the same persistent problem as his father had known. How to control such a huge region with a number of knights which declined dramatically in the autumn when the crusaders returned home after their forty day period of fighting?

At the start of 1219, Amaury laid siege to Marmande while, at the same time, Montpellier and Nimes lent their support to Raymond VI and his son.

In view of the gravity of the situation, the King of France intervened through his son Louis with a large contingent of knights and archers. The massacre of Marmande was carried out in his name, an event perpetrated deliberately after the town was taken (May 1219). Louis decided to withdraw from the rest of the events of the crusade after the failure of the siege of Toulouse, with the exception of his mandatory forty-day period.

The revolt continued and gained ground and Amaury gradually lost all the territories to Raymond VII, whose father (Raymond VI) had died in August 1222. Attempts at peace between the two parties failed, but, finally, an agreement was signed in front of Carcassonne between the Counts of Toulouse and Foix and Amaury de Montfort (January 1224). The first crusade was over and after so much destruction, death and suffering, the situation appeared to be exactly the same as it had been in 1208 (even the son of the Viscount of Béziers-Carcassonne, Trencavel had recovered his land).

The coat-of-arms of Amaury de Montfort, Simon de Montfort's eldest son.

Document from the 16th century, extract from *Recueil des Rois de France* by Jean de Tillet. Bibliothèque Nationale, Paris. Ms fr. 2848, f° 204 v°.

Amaury de Montfort

Simon de Montfort's eldest son. In 1213 he married the only daughter of André of Burgundy, heir of Dauphiné; on the death of his father in 1218, he took over military operations but found himself faced with an increasingly difficult situation. In 1226, Amaury transferred all his rights over the conquered territories to the King of France and became his constable in 1227. In 1239 he was forced to renounce his rights over the County of Leicester in England (relic of the Norman conquest). Finally, after many adventures and dramas, he found himself no more than the lord of the seigniory owned by his father in Ile-de-France before setting out to fight the Cathars. He took part in the crusade to the Holy Land in 1242 and was taken prisoner outside Gaza. He was freed two years later after the Pope paid the ransom and he died on his return in Otranto (at the tip of the Italian "boot").

The massacre of Marmande (May 1219)

The massacre of Marmande was carried out by the French crusaders under conditions very similar to those of the massacre of Béziers in 1209. Again, the idea was to generate terror, but this time the decision was premeditated and debated in council prior to the attack, particularly with Simon de Monfort's son, Amaury, who had a terrible desire for vengeance after the death of his father outside Toulouse. About 5,000 people perished in the presence of Prince Louis, the son of Philip Augustus.

"[...] Lords, ladies and their little children, women and men stripped naked, all these men slashed and cut to pieces with keen-edged swords. Flesh, blood and brains, trunks, limbs and faces hacked in two, lungs, livers and guts torn out and tossed aside on the open ground as if they had rained down from the sky. Marshland and good ground, all was red with blood. Not a man or a woman was left alive, neither old nor young, no living creature, unless any had managed to hide. Marmande was razed and set alight."

Extract from *La Chanson de la Croisade Albigeoise* by William of Tudela, chapter CCXII, 9306-9321.

The Porte d'Aude gate in the walled town of Carcassonne.

Text from the agreement which marked the end of the first crusade against the Albigensians

(signed outside Carcassonne on 14 January 1224)

"Here are the conventions passed between us, the Counts of Toulouse and Foix on the one hand and Count Amaury and his men on the other hand.

On the subject of the promises we have made in order to obtain peace for the Holy Roman Church and Count Amaury, the latter must consult his friends from France, do what they advise him to do, work in good faith to ensure that peace is obtained between the Church and his own people, not place any obstacles in our way, and give us a reply before next Whitsun (3 June) as to what should be done on this matter.

Until then, all the churches will remain as they are and keep in peace all that they own, especially the Lord Bishop of Narbonne and his suffragan bishops, the Lord Bishop of Agen, all the other prelates in the region and the clerics, regardless of where they are.

Narbonne, Agde, Penne d'Albigeois, La Roque de Valsergue, Termes, and all the land held by Amaury, or which is held in his name, with the exception of Carcassonne, Minerve and Penne d'Agenais, are protected by the truce for the following two months. This means that we will not attack or allow any attack on the property or people who hold these castles and towns. We

Lastours Castle.
This site, north of Carcassonne, is unusual in that it has four castles. It was a centre of Cathar court life and a refuge during the crusaders' forays.

will only recover these castles and lands if it is the wish of those who protect them and who inhabit them.
We will be entitled to enter Narbonne and Agde as many times as we wish, on the condition that we do not violate the rights of the churches or the inhabitants of these towns, or carry out any violence, and we will not recover our rights over these towns before a period of two months.
We must return their heritage to the knights and all those have been dispossessed for supporting Count Amaury, especially the inhabitants of Béziers, Narbonne and Carcassonne, as well as Amanieu d'Albret, Raymond de Capendu, Raymond-Bernard de Rovignan, Bérenger de Montlaur, the Countess of Rodez and her son, and Raymond-Arnaud de Saissac, to the best of our ability, without violence and in good faith. We will not fault them for having supported the Count's cause, provided, however, that they swear loyalty to us and remain loyal to us.
Finally, we promise to give Count Amaury, within the timescale defined by him and by us, ten thousand marks in cash, if he obtains complete peace for us and our allies from the Church."
***Histoire Générale de Languedoc* by Dom Vaissère, Privat, 1872 and the years that followed, VIII, n° 229.**

But, the papacy could not be content with an agreement which was no more than a sign of its defeat, and the new Pope, Honorius III asked the new King of France, Louis VIII, to take up the flag of the crusade once again. He did so before the agreement of Carcassonne had even been signed in December 1223.

Towards a second crusade

In order to intervene in and lead a crusade, Louis VIII (February 1224) laid out several conditions which reveal the fundamentally political nature of his involvement. Nothing much has been remembered about the life and acts of this King who ruled between two emblematic sovereigns, Philip Augustus and Saint Louis, but he, too, had the same idea as the other Kings of France which was to extend the original royal territory of Ile-de-France.

Louis VIII asked (among other things) that the Pope obtain the extension of the truce with the King of England for him, the written confirmation of the transfer to him of the

land that had been confiscated and the appointment of the Archbishop of Toulouse as legate.

Naturally, the Pope could not accept these conditions because it would have meant an end to the Church's independent action in the Albigensian region and, more seriously, the loss of what had been obtained by the Popes in terms of theocracy. After some consideration and discussions with Raymond VII, who, naturally, was unhappy about the prospect of a new crusade, in April, the Pope declared that he was abandoning his idea of a crusade against the Albigensians in order to focus his efforts on a crusade in the Holy Land in which Frederick II, the German Roman Emperor, would participate (the person whom Pope Innocent III and King Philip Augustus had supported against his competitor Otto). Louis VIII took note of this change of heart.

These reversals have intrigued historians and various explanations have been put forward to justify them. In terms of the actual facts, it is obvious that the Pope's new position lent support to Raymond VII and opposed the desire of the French to seize control of Languedoc.

Diplomatic manoeuvring, proposals and counter-proposals, official and secret negotiations, all the procedures between the conflict's stakeholders (papacy, Count of Toulouse, Simon de Montfort's son, King of France) lasted nearly two years and led to a Council in Bourges which saw several unexpected developments.

Régine Tower in Lastours Castle.

Top:
Meeting between Philip II, called Philip Augustus, and a bishop (1188).
Extract from *Les Grandes Chroniques de France*, manuscript from 1335. London, British Library. AKG-Images.

The conditions laid out by Louis VIII to lead the crusade against the heretics (February 1224)

"The King requests that he and all those who go with him to the Albigensian region benefit from the same indulgence and remission of sins as those for overseas Crusaders.

Item – The King requests that the Archbishops of Bourges, Reims and Sens are granted full powers to excommunicate people and cast interdict on the lands of all those, from the Kingdom of France or abroad, who threaten or attack the King of France or the people or lands of those who travel with him, as well as those who fight against each other within the Kingdom of France, unless, on order of the King, they agree to peace or a truce.

Item – The King requests that the aforementioned archbishops are given the power to force, by excommunication and interdict, those who undertake to travel with him to the Albigensian region or remain there, to pay the agreed sums.

Item – The King requests that these are given the power to excommunicate people and cast interdict on the lands of the lords of France and their other vassals who choose not to, or who are unable to travel with him to the Albigensian region, and who do not pay a sufficient fee to hunt down Albigen-

sians, enemies of the Faith and of the Kingdom. They are obliged by homage and oath to serve the King against the enemies of the Kingdom and the Kingdom has no greater enemy than the enemies of Faith. The aforementioned sentences may only be lifted after the necessary settlement.
Item – The King wishes and requests that the truce, as required by the Pope, the King of Jerusalem and the King of England, is renewed for a ten year period between himself and his heirs, and the King of England and his heirs [...] because the King does not know how long this affair will last and how much it will cost him and the Kingdom in money and men.
Item – The King requests that the Lord Pope confirms in writing the confiscation of the County of Toulouse, the Viscountcy of Béziers and Carcassonne, all the kingdom's lands belonging to those who have fought openly with or for them, as well as all those who oppose or who have opposed this affair and who are or have been involved in the fighting. That all the afore-mentioned lands are transferred in perpetuity to him and his heirs and to those to whom he wishes to grant them, subject to homage being paid to him and to his heirs as their superior lord.

A heretic escorted by a monk on his way to trial.
These Inquisition scenes were already common at the time of the fight against the Cathars.
Detail from a painting by Pedro Berruguete, auto-da-fé presided over by Saint Dominic.
The Art Archive/Musée du Prado/Dagli Orti.

Item – The King requests that the Archbishop of Bourges is granted to him as legate, with, among other powers, that of reconciling all those who meet the Church's requirements.
Item – With expenses being vast and difficult to estimate, the King requests that, every year, for a ten-year period, the Roman Church grants him sixty thousand livres parisis to be used for the benefit of this country.
If all these articles are guaranteed and confirmed to the King, the King will travel in person to the Albigensian region to work in good faith in this affair. The Roman Curia must leave him and his heirs the freedom to remain in the region, and to travel to and fro as he wishes.
In order to present these requests to the Roman Curia and have them approved, the King sends his loyal supporters, the Archbishop of Bourges and the Bishops of Langres and Chartres. If these requests are not accepted, the King will only be obliged to go to the Albigensian region if he wishes to do so."
Histoire Générale du Languedoc by Dom Vaissère, VIII, n° 236.

Inquisition tribunal presided over by Saint Dominic in 1220.
The effectiveness of the Inquisition came largely from the terror which the institution prompted.
Painting by Pedro Berruguete (1495). Madrid, Prado Museum. AKG-Images.

The "French solution" (1226-1229)

Finally, in January 1228, Louis VIII succeeded in having a parliament, comprising all the main seigniorial families in France (27 representatives), archbishops (5) and bishops (many), adopt the principle of a crusade which would lead to the conviction of Raymond VII by the legate, the transfer to Louis VIII of all the Count of Toulouse's rights over the Albigensian region and the official devolution of these lands to Louis VIII. This was not stated clearly in the text which is, in some respects, the French clergy's manifesto in support of the crusade. However, all the religious and legal conditions had been brought together to guarantee that this crusade would ensure the territorial expansion of the Kingdom of France in Occitania.

The troops gathered in Bourges in the middle of May. The simple announcement of the arrival of the royal forces, which Philip Augustus, with the recent victory in the Battle of the Bouvines (1214), had given a special prestige, spread terror through the towns and the lords who, shortly before, had sworn loyalty to Raymond VII. The route followed by the crusade was the same as in 1209, but the scale of the forces involved was much greater.

It is easy to be confused by the repeated and often contradictory oaths taken by the towns and the lords in support of the opposing sides in such a short space of time. Some have suggested that the religious foundation of the Occitan rebellion, namely the Cathar religion, had been greatly weakened. However, documents analysed by a leading specialist in the subject, Michel Roquebert (see bibliography at the end of the book), show that, in 1226, in Pieusse-en-Razès near Limoux, a Cathar council was held which decided to establish a Cathar bishop in Razès in addition to the other four already in place. Therefore, the weakened state of the Cathar church does not appear to be a good explanation, nor does the one of pure and simple fear. Was it not quite simply the idea that the arrival of a prince as powerful and legendary as the King of France would, at long last, ensure lasting peace, even if it meant that the Occitan identity would lose a little of its sub-

Siege of the town of Avignon.
The town had initially agreed to receive the crusade, but later opposed it.
It capitulated in September 1226.
Document from the 15th century, extract from *Les Grandes Chroniques de France* by Jean Fouquet. Bibliothèque Nationale, Paris, Ms fr. 6465 f° 251 v°.

stance? Also, the diplomatic preparation of this crusade had been effective and Louis VIII was certain that neither the King of Aragon, nor the King of England would intervene.

The foray of Louis VIII (May to November 1226)

From March 1226 onwards, the number of people switching sides and the number of oaths of loyalty grew, but Raymond VII, too, increased the number of acts through which he, his vassals and the towns would undertake to resist the crusade and the King of France. One particular volte-face would have a great impact: that of Avignon which, firstly, had expressed its wish to play host to the crusade, but which, once it arrived at the start of June, organised a strong resistance, even more difficult to quash since the town of Avignon was part of Imperial Germany and Emperor Frederick II had no real reason, in fact, quite the contrary, to meet any demands by the papacy. Finally, Avignon capitulated in September 1226.

Declaration by the major prelates of France at the start of the second crusade against the Albigensians (January 1228)

"With Louis, illustrious King of the French, being in charge of the affair of the Cross against the Albigensian heretics which aims to root out the heretic perversion, we have taken under the protection of the Church himself, his family, his Kingdom and all those who travel and work alongside him in this affair for as long as they are at the service of Christ.
By the authority of the all-powerful Lord, Saint Peter and Saint Paul and our own, we grant them the same indulgence as for crusaders in the Holy Land, as stipulated by the Council of the Lateran.
We have excommunicated and condemned as excommunicated Raymond, son of Raymond, formerly Count of Toulouse, his supporters, his accomplices and all those who have lent him council against the Church, the Christian faith and the King of France, who works to defend this faith.
We also excommunicate all those who attack or invade the Kingdom of France, whether they are from within the Kingdom or from overseas. Nobody will be relieved of the sentence of excommunication unless that have given satisfaction to the King and his subjects for any wrong or damage, and unless the overseas warring parties or invaders have left the Kingdom.
We also excommunicate all those from the Kingdom of France who fight among themselves, unless they agree to a truce or peace following the orders of the Lord King."
***Histoire Générale du Languedoc* by Dom Vaissère, VIII, n° 244-1.**

However, this respite, or rather this delay, in the foray did allow Louis VIII to obtain a large number of new oaths of loyalty: Nimes, Castres, Carcassonne. After the fall of Avignon, Louis VIII made a very important decision to create a bailiwick (meaning a civil and military government, a royal authority, therefore, outside the feudal framework), with its seat at Beaucaire Castle, an act which clearly showed his desire to simply incorporate all of lower Languedoc (Beaucaire, Nimes) into the royal kingdom of France. It was also at this moment that, in order to get around the major difficulty of not being able to establish a French military garrison in Avignon (part of the Empire), he founded the fortress that was going to become Villeneuve-lès-Avignon (he had it built with money paid by the defeated town of Avignon).

The forays started again: Béziers, Carcassonne (with the creation of another royal bailiwick, that of Béziers-Carcassonne), Pamiers, Castelnaudary, Puilaurens, Lavaur, Albi. Very tired and ill, Louis VIII died on his return to Montpensier (8 November 1226), but not without having appointed the leader of the army who was going to remain in place, Humbert de Beaujeu.

Surrender of Avignon (1226), on the left, and coronation of Louis IX, on the right.

Extract from *Les Grandes Chroniques de France de Charles V*, in around 1375-1380. Bibliothèque Nationale, Paris, Ms fr. 2813, f° 266 v°.

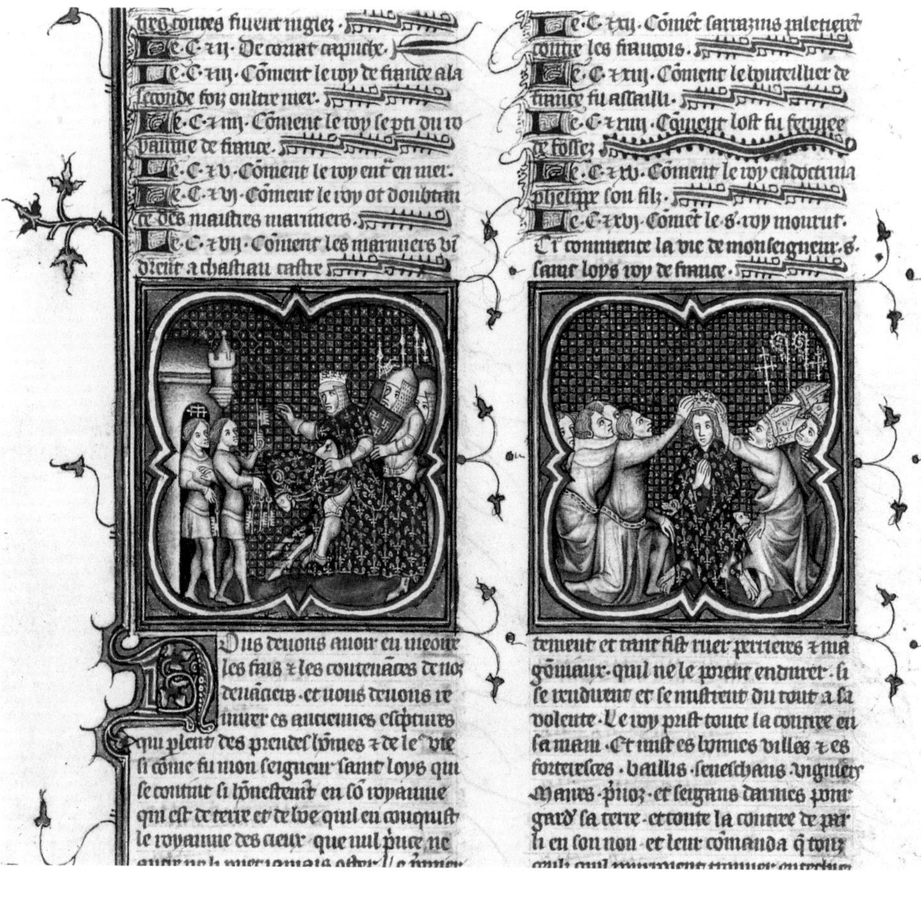

This foray, which appears to have achieved its initial goals, took place within an entirely different context from the first crusade in political and legal terms. It is true that the King was surrounded by his main vassals, who, themselves, were accompanied by their own vassals, but the decisions taken by the King, including that of appointing a military leader, was part of a different framework from that of the feudal system. It was a sovereign, a Head of State, an architect of centralisation and the strengthening of centralised power, who had taken the initiative.

Humbert de Beaujeu

This representative of Louis VIII, and later of Louis IX, in the Albigensian region from 1226 onwards, came from a noble family from the region of Villefranche. His father, Guichard IV the Great, died in 1216 at the siege of Douvres, after accompanying Prince Louis (future Louis VIII) on his Albigensian crusade. Hubert or Humbert V led the French army in the Albigensian region, especially during the siege of Montségur. Very little is known about him other than the fact that he later accompanied Baudoin de Courtenay to Constantinople and that Saint Louis made him a constable. He died in the Holy Land in 1250.

Renewed fighting

Almost immediately after the death of Louis VIII, the rebellion erupted. The regent Blanche of Castile (in this position because the son she had had with Louis VIII was still a minor) had very few means at her disposal to quash it because some major vassals, not from the North, intended to take advantage of the regency to oppose centralised royal power.

The rebellion escalated and once again, the oaths that had been taken proved to be illusory. Although the events involved small-scale fighting and refusals to pay the royal tax, they did create a difficult situation in which the Cathar church played a major role. The height of the crisis came when Raymond VII entered the conflict. Naturally, this led to a new excommunication for the Count of Toulouse and the renewed withdrawal of his feudal rights, etc. Humbert de Beaujeu attempted to control the revolt in some areas through the use of the habitual destruction, massacre and barbaric acts, while Raymond VII extended his empire. The seigniories and towns were occupied one after another by the opposing sides and it was always the population which found itself having to pay the price of these changing situations (eyewitness accounts from the period talk of the systematic destruction of crops, especially vineyards, by the French troops).

The French forces grew in strength over summer 1228 (still with the seasonal problem of ost), and, no doubt, influenced the attempts of both sides to find a peaceful solution.

In Albi, Pont Vieux, Sainte-Cécile Cathedral and La Berbie Palace.

Right:
Montségur Castle: emblematic site of the crusaders' fight against the Cathars.

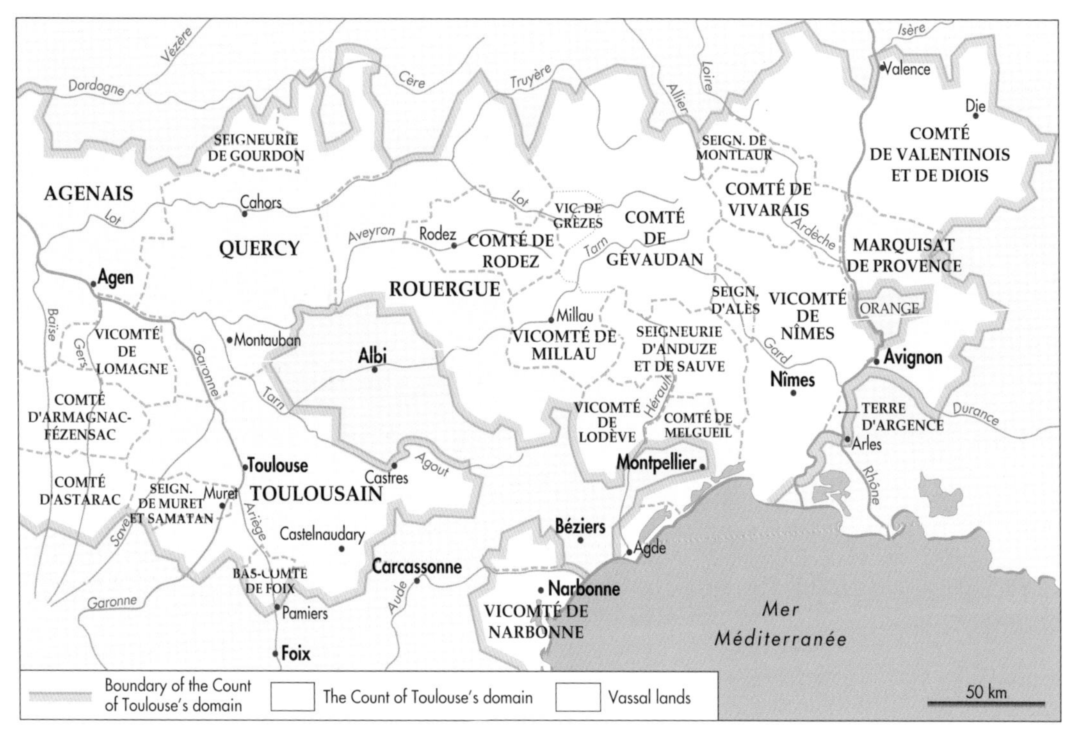

The Count of Toulouse's States prior to the Treaty of Paris (1229).

The Treaty of Paris

Negotiations were not easy and, above all, they were clouded by an event which is still unclear. Discussions started at the end of 1228 with an initial project proposed by France at the start of 1229. A conference bringing together both sides was organised in Meaux (a town outside of the royal kingdom of Ile-de-France) based on this project, which, in the meantime, had become much more severe, and the Count of Toulouse was forced to submit (although, initially, he had wanted to lessen the severity of the text).

The outcome of this meeting was what is known as the Treaty of Paris (12 April 1229) a basic document which marks if not the end of the Cathar problem (because this was still a distant hope as we will see later), at least an end to Occitan political autonomy. A page had been turned and a very important step had been taken in the history of the Kingdom of France. Therefore, it is interesting to take a brief look at what this treaty involved.

Let us start by examining something which may appear strange to modern-day readers. Raymond VII had already been accused of supporting heresy in the past, yet there is no suggestion of a withdrawal of this accusation, or of a trial. This might suggest that the main aspect of the situation was political and not religious, as we have been led to believe (but such irony would not be appropriate in view of the countless deaths) as much from papal declarations as from the massacre and destruction carried out in its name.

Therefore, the main aspect of the treaty is political:

— the transfer by the Count of more than half of his land to the King, namely the present-day territories of Gard, Hérault, part of Aude, Tarn and Ariège;

— the Count's continued control over the

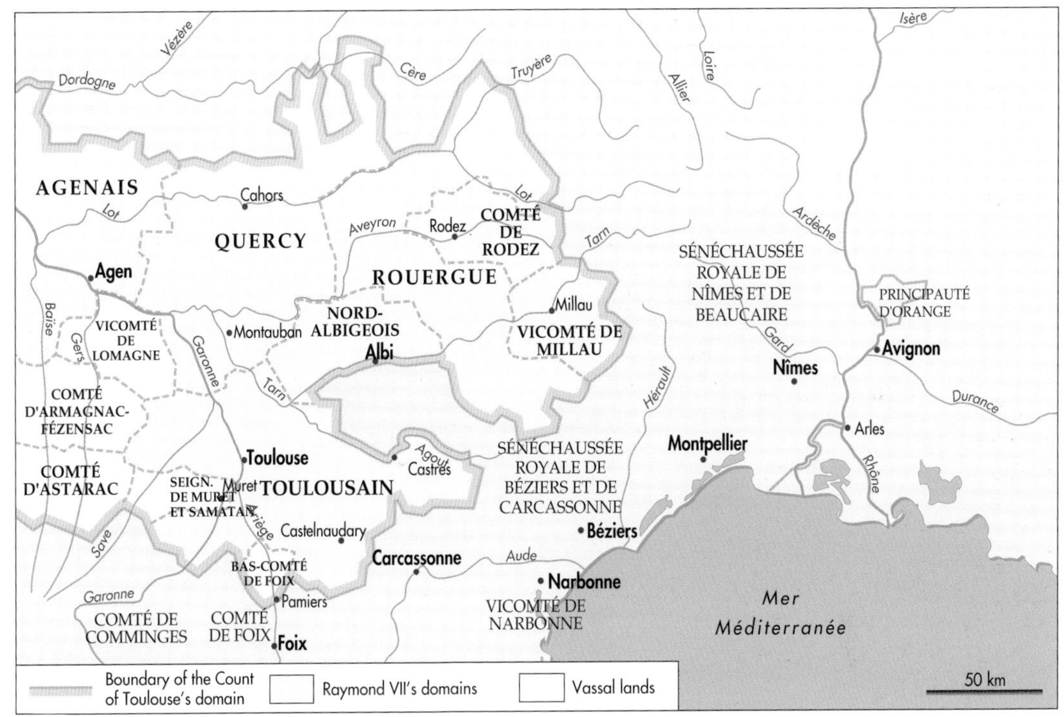

The States of the Count of Toulouse after the Treaty of Paris (1229).

remaining area (Tarn, Tarn-et-Garonne, Haute-Garonne, Aveyron) under a form of a life annuity, because through the arranged marriage between the Count's only daughter and the brother of the King of France, Alphonse of Poitiers, it was agreed that on the death of the latter, everything would revert to France, even if the couple had a son (their two children were born in 1220) or if Joan was widowed and remarried.

This proposed wedding, whose main and even sole purpose was political, was also a family affair. Eleanor of Aquitaine, Louis VII's first wife, had had two daughters: Eleanor, the mother of Blanche of Castile, therefore, the grandmother of Alfonso of Poitiers, and Joan of England, the grandmother of Joan of Toulouse. Also, Alfonso of Poitiers was the great-grandson of Louis VII, whose sister Constance had been the wife of Raymond V of Toulouse, therefore, she was the great-grandmother of Joan of Toulouse (Raymond VII and the regent Blanche of Castile were cousins). The wedding took place in 1237.

— recovery by the Count of all his feudal rights (therefore, cancellation of the donations made by Simon de Montfort and his son Amaury) in return for the Count's allegiance to Louis IX;

— general and reciprocal amnesty;

— dismantling of the fortifications of more than thirty towns and castles, including Toulouse.

Defeated and bound, the Count of Toulouse was also exposed to two humiliations: that of canonical reconciliation (the same as his father in Saint-Gilles in 1209) and being taken prisoner and held in the Louvre for several weeks while the French authorities took control of the castles and started dismantling the fortifications.

The men of the court of the Inquisition (1150). This cold scene reflects particularly well the feeling of anxiety inspired by the Inquisition.
Painting by Jean-Paul Laurens, 1889. Moulins, Musée d'Art et d'Archéologie. AKG-Images/Erich Lessing.

The strengthening of the Cathar repression

Although in the text of the Treaty of Paris, purely religious questions were somewhat forgotten, it must not be thought that these no longer counted. Two texts completed the legal framework for fighting the Cathars, because, as we will see shortly, there were still many supporters of the Cathar faith during the period following the signature of the Treaty prior to the advent of new dramas.

The first of these texts dates from May 1226 and was signed by Louis VIII. He transferred the sentencing of heretics from religious canonical law to secular civil law:

"We have decided that heretics who stray from the Catholic faith, regardless of the name given to them, once sentenced for heresy by the bishop or by any other person of the Church with the relevant power, will receive the deserved punishment immediately. We order and decree that whoever dares to open their doors to heretics, support them or provide them with any form of help will not be heard, allowed any form of dignity, or the right to make a will, or benefit from an inheritance. Such a person's movables and immovables will be confiscated and may not under any circumstances be recovered by him or his descendants…"

Some concrete measures implemented in the fight against the Cathars (according to the Council of Toulouse in 1229 and the edict of Raymond VII in 1233)

– Destruction of houses where heretics have lived or preached.
– Obligation for penitents to wear the cross of penitence on their clothing.
– Obligation for all inhabitants over the age of 12 years for women and 14 years for men to swear to their Catholic faith, to the desire to denounce heretics and to repeat the oath every two years.
– Obligation to confess and receive communion three times a year (Christmas, Easter, Whitsun).
– Obligation to take part in mass on Sundays and on religious holidays (a total of 94 days in the year).
– Ban on having the Old and the New Testament at home, even in Latin.
– Ban on making a will without the presence of a priest or a monk.

The Cathar heresy and the Inquisition

The Inquisition's actions against the Cathars really got under way in 1233. The Pope Gregory IX appointed the Archbishop of Vienne (in France) as legate in the provinces of Languedoc, the region of Bordeaux and Catalonia, etc., with full powers to eradicate heresy, without being answerable to the bishop or to the civil authorities. The legate transferred these far-reaching powers, via the Bishops of Toulouse and Albi, to two preaching brothers (Dominicans) who were the first Inquisitors, namely Pierre Seila (from Toulouse) and Guillaume Arnaud (from Montpellier).

The efficiency of the Inquisition courts was based mainly on the terror which they inspired by not following the standard rules of criminal procedure. According to them, a person could only be prosecuted in three cases: either the prosecutor in charge of the preliminary enquiry had gathered proof of the offence or crime, or a denunciation based on eyewitness accounts had been made to the judge, or the offence had been public and manifest with eyewitness accounts testifying to its public and manifest nature.

In the case of the Cathars, the first and third mechanism did not enter into play, either out of fear or solidarity. Therefore, the Inquisition mainly used the second option, but made it much easier.

In actual fact, in line with normal criminal procedure, people who, in the past, had already harmed or insulted the accused, as well as family members, servants and all those who depended on him, excommunicated people and heretics, were excluded from the right to denounce. The Inquisition removed these restrictions, therefore, opening the way to a flow of denunciations which may have been motivated by self interest. Also, the procedure used was improved by two other measures with devastating effects: if a lawyer defended a heretic, this made him a potential suspect of heresy (which explains the increased number of trials without defence lawyers), and, the hearing of witnesses (almost all dependents) were held in camera and often without the presence of the accused.

The increase in the number of denunciations, the procedures followed by the Inquisitors who, on the basis of a denunciation, would interrogate the accused to find out who he had seen (and where) behaving as a Perfect or a simple Cathar believer and the use of torture (legalised by bull from Innocent IV in 1252), all contributed to creating a climate of terror in Languedoc.

In April 1229, when the Treaty of Paris was signed, Louis IX signed another text which completes this first one by adding a new essential element. The Occitan vassals, owing to their vassalic homage to the King of France, had to become involved in the fight against heretics and participate in hunting them down. This meant that there was complete confusion between religious aspects (ecclesiastical) and civil aspects (secular):

"We have decided and decreed that the lords of the land, our officers and our other present and future subjects, are required to work with the greatest care to purge the land of heretics and of the corruption of heresy."

The interesting point of this text was the fact that royal "officers" (the equivalent of modern-day civil servants) were now going to become involved in the fight against the Cathars.

Montségur, the stone commemorating the execution by fire.
Photo J. Debru.

Right:
Montségur: the "pog" and the castle.
Photo J. Debru.

Montségur, the end of the Cathars (1244)

Montségur: this very name is heavy in meaning. The deaths by fire on 16 March 1244, after a very long siege, remain in the collective memory as a symbol of the Cathar tragedy and it was in reference to Montségur that the ideas mentioned at the start of this book gained ground (the "Cathar's treasure", Montségur solar temple, Montségur, a relay point for religions from India, Montségur and the Grail, etc.).

Fortunately, in recent decades, research on Montségur has been based on more scientific developments. One of the slightly paradoxical results of this research has been that some of the most interesting ideas by N. Peyrat, the great apologist of the Albigensian adventure in the second half of the 19th century, have been viewed in a harsher light now that the documents and places are better known.

Apart from these differences in viewpoints, it is clear that the siege, defeat, and deaths by fire at Montségur are a key chronological reference point. After 1244, Catharism was in its final death throes and only survived a short time.

The Inquisition procedures

The word inquisition, from Latin inquirere, meaning to enquire, inform about, is heavy in meaning. There is uncertainty about the exact date of its establishment because, on the one hand, we know the texts of the Fourth Council of the Lateran (1215) which plan for the systematic handing over of heretics to the secular authorities, and, on the other hand, the activity of Dominic who, in 1215, also created the Order of Preachers. But, we know that Dominic was not the first Inquisitor. It is reasonable to assume that the functioning of the Inquisition and its affirmation as an original and independent organisation gained ground during the Cathar crusade, with the development of procedures which were materialised in the texts dating from after 1230. It was not until the first quarter of the 19th century that the Inquisi-

tion ceased to exist, meaning the procedures, which, remember, were refined over the centuries with the description we have given not necessarily corresponding to practices at the time of the fight against the Cathars.
Behind a trial there was almost always a denunciation. The Inquisition court announced its arrival in a given town or village in advance, informing the population that it had three days to accuse themselves or accuse others, at the risk of excommunication. The psychological effect of such an announcement could be referred to as "devastating spying". If the denunciation was recognised as being founded by the Inquisition's prosecutor (without any contradictory debate or the presence of a lawyer), it led to an arrest and the person being held in solitary confinement. Then the trial started: the accused was informed that a witness had seen him doing this or that, without giving the name of the witness, and, normally, without the presence of a lawyer (a lawyer who knowingly helped a heretic risked excommunication himself as well as the accusation of being a heretic). The use of torture was also possible: forced ingestion of large quantities of water, burning of feet, thighs, legs and arms fastened tightly with rope. The accused was able to cite counter witnesses (to clear his name). At the end of the trial, which could last several months, the court pronounced the acquittal (very rarely) or the sentence: penitence, prison, flagellation, exile, confiscation of property, ban from exercising a profession. The accused was then handed over to the secular authorities for the sentence to be carried out.
It was in Spain that the Inquisition imposed its greatest authority, thus explaining the term "auto de fe" which some wrongly associate with death by fire. In actual fact, this was the "act of faith" pronounced by the Inquisition when the sentence was made in public as proof of a person's attachment to the faith.
It is easy to imagine the impact of these measures on the population. A mechanism which, necessarily, would give rise to terror, rebellion and repression was in place.

Death by fire at Montségur (1226). The most common sentence for heretics was death by fire either handed down by the Inquisition or carried out at the end of a siege.
Wood engraving (1880) based on a drawing by Emile Bayard. AKG-Images.

Landscape in the Montagne Noire: Carcassès and the Pic de Nore.

The situation in the region after the Treaty of Paris

Undoubtedly, the Treaty of Paris gave the religious authorities the power to eradicate the Cathar heresy. In November 1229, a Council was held in Toulouse at the initiative of the legate, the Roman cardinal Frangipani. The text produced by this council, a proper administrative circular to use a modern term, laid out the concrete and precise powers of a new institution which, in each province would comprise a priest and a few laymen in charge of unearthing suspects, denouncing them and searching their property, etc. A genuine police state was set up throughout the country. In short, the Inquisition was born, although its character had altered slightly coming under the control of a religious order and no longer being the responsibility of the bishops.

Very soon, Cathar followers executed some of their own who were among the members of these search teams. The royal seneschal André Chaulet was also assassinated. A menacing atmosphere spread. The attitude of the Count of Toulouse, Raymond VII, was, as was frequently the case, very ambiguous and his relations with the Bishop of Toulouse, Fulk, in position for more than twenty years, clearly highlight this ambiguity. Over time, the Bishop, a long-time and almost frenzied supporter of the Cathar repression, had become more reconciling. Fulk's death (in 1231) and his replacement by Raymond of Fauga changed the situation, with the new bishop deciding to be harsher and firmer with the Count in order to ensure that he truly became involved in the fight against the heretics. He succeeded in having Raymond VII take part in a foray in the Montagne Noire.

The Count, pressed and even harassed by those who wanted him to apply the terms of the Treaty of Paris for hunting down heretics, prepared and promulgated (in April 1233) an edict which planned in detail the policing measures (there is no other more suitable term) to be employed in this hunt.

In 1233, the Pope (Gregory IX) assigned preaching brothers (Dominicans) to pursue

Fulk, Bishop of Toulouse (1155-1231)

Originally a trader, a husband and the father of two children, he entered the Order of Cîteaux in 1195, as part of Thoronet Abbey, of which he became the abbot in 1199. He was elected Bishop of Toulouse by the cathedral's chapter in 1205. He was a very active bishop, implementing the papal instructions designed to instil order in terms of the conduct of priests and preaching, and became famous for his anti-Cathar fanaticism.

His methods were different from those of Arnaud-Amaury, the Abbot of Cîteaux and Archbishop of Narbonne, who had very material ambitions on the Duchy of Narbonne. Fulk set up a genuine private militia, the White Brotherhood, which attacked Jews and heretics, and he regularly found himself in conflict with the Count of Toulouse. He took part in the preparation of the Treaty of Paris and closely monitored its application by organising the Council of Toulouse.

Cathar heretics before Saint Dominic.
Saint Dominic actively fought heresy, especially the Cathar heresy.
Saint Dominic's tomb, marble relief by Nicolas Pisano.
The Art Archive/Basilica of San Domenico/Dagli Orti.

Saint Dominic (around 1170-1221)

Michelet said of this founder of the Inquisition that "nobody had a greater gift for tears than him, something often associated with fanaticism". In all cases, his life and work were closely linked to the Cathar tragedy. Born in Castile to a noble family in around 1170, Dominique de Guzman was elected canon of Osma Cathedral in 1196 and, in 1203, accompanied his bishop on a journey to Denmark (which is not certain to have taken place, but, the two travellers did go to Rome).
It was at this moment, when passing through Toulouse, that he saw the progress made by the heretics. This experience had an effect on Dominic, who asked to be relieved of his vow as canon and to remain there in order to preach, which he did from 1205 to 1215. In 1206, he founded a convent for Cathar women who had abjured in Prouille near Toulouse.
At the start of the armed crusade (1209), Dominic joined forces with Simon de Montfort (it was he who married Simon's eldest son, Amaury). Thanks to a sizeable donation made to him by a bourgeois from Toulouse, he created a convent and obtained the Pope's authorisation to create a preaching order which he led until his death in 1221.

heretics and to create what were to become the courts of the Inquisition. These were implemented very quickly and the fanaticism they involved led to an explosion among the population.

The event, in some respects the catalyst, was macabre. With a view to spreading terror (showing the population what could happen after death in the case of heresy), the Dominicans decided to exhume the bodies of people who had been identified as heretics after their death and burn them in public. Such extreme measures created huge emotion and were a source of riots, as was the case, in particular, in Albi in 1234.

The attitude of Raymond VII, ambiguous as we have already seen, continues to surprise us in view of the situation faced by the population for whom he was still the sovereign (although, only under an annuity) and the political manoeuvring in which he was engaged. Above all, he was thinking of his own interests and, especially, the recovery of his lands in Provence which were part of the empire, helping to explain his manoeuvres with Emperor Fredrick II who was in conflict with the Pope. During this time, the conflict grew between the Inquisitors, the local religious and civil authorities and the population. One particularly striking example was the expulsion of Dominican monks by the municipality of Toulouse in the absence of Raymond VII.

Pope Gregory IX entrusts the Dominicans with fighting heretics.
Because of the role it played in the Inquisition, the Dominican Order has often been identified with this event, but this is not entirely correct. Originally, this order undertook to fight heresy mainly through preaching. But, it is true that it was this Order that the Pope entrusted with the mission of finding and fighting heretics by all available means (scene depicted by this document).
Bibliothèque Sainte-Geneviève, photo Etel.

Saint Peter of Verona.
A former Cathar heretic, Saint Peter of Verona converted to the official Catholic doctrine very early on. He became a Dominican friar and was one of the most feared Inquisitors sentencing a large number of Cathars to death by fire. He was canonised two years after his death as a hero of the fight against heresy.
Bibliothèque Nationale, Paris, Ms fr. 277, f° 135 v°.

Of course, the Pope protested and accused (rightly) the Count of not respecting his undertakings and enjoined him to leave for the Holy Land in Easter 1237, something the Count refused to do. Also, the conflict between the Pope and Emperor Frederick II started to resemble a military campaign, opening up new opportunities for Raymond VII. But, the war was going to start again in the Albigensian region (in the widest sense of the term) with the arrival in force of Raymond II Trencavel, whose father, the Viscount of Béziers and Carcassonne, had been one of Simon de Montfort's first victims (remember that he was killed in 1209). The Viscount's lands were incorporated into the French royal domain in 1119. In summer 1240, Raymond II Trencavel set out on a new campaign to win back these lands, supported by the population's rebellion and a large part of the nobility from his former viscountcy. He travelled as far as Carcassonne, which he laid siege to in September 1240, but which he was unable to take because Louis IX had sent more troops. To escape, Trencavel sought refuge in Montréal before travelling to Spain. The revolt ended in failure, and, once again, the land of the "Albigensians" found itself ravaged by the royal troops.

Montségur at the forefront of history

The site of Montségur lies east of Foix and southwest of Carcassonne in the region of Olmes, in the seigniory of Mirepoix, called the "Terre du Maréchal", an area of land alongside one (viscountcy of Béziers and Carcassonne) already annexed to France in 1229.

Very little is known about the history of the site before 1204. It was around this date that one of the two lords of Montségur, Raymond of Péreille, declared to the Inquisitors, after the fall of the castle: "on the persistent requests and prayers of Raymond of Mirepoix, Raymond Blasco and other heretics, I rebuilt the castrum of Montségur, which, until then, had been in ruins [...] forty years ago and more".

The word "castrum" has a very clear meaning and refers to a fortified castle. Excavation work carried out since 1950 has helped to find more than a few reminders of this period, although, naturally, the French royal forces proceeded with the destruction of these fortifications after the capitulation in 1244.

Montségur covered in snow.
Photo R. Cast.

Many documents testify to the fact that after 1204, Montségur Castle was an active centre of the Cathar faith. At the start of the first crusade, an important Cathar prelate, Guilhabert of Castres, established himself there and at the Council of the Lateran in 1215, the name of Montségur was cited as being a centre for heretics and the Count of Toulouse is reproached for not having done anything to prevent its expansion.

The Treaty of Paris (1229) clearly strengthened Montségur's role as a refuge. This castle belonged to two lords, but one of them, Pierre-Roger of Mirepoix, first cousin and also son-in-law of the other, was much more active in religious matters. This explains why, in 1232, Guilhabert of Castres asked that Montségur become the "seat and the head" (domicilium and caput) of the persecuted Cathar church. Many interrogations by the Inquisitors, analysed with devotion and finesse by Michel Roquebert, provide an insight into the activity of the bishops and Cathar Perfects based at Montségur.

Guilhabert of Castres
(born in around 1165, died in around 1240)

Cathar theologian, he took part in major debates in the first decade of the 13th century between priests and religious experts from both sides. At the start of the first crusade, he took refuge in Montségur, which had just been rebuilt. In 1233, he established the "seat and head" of the Cathar church there, of which he was one of the highest dignitaries (he was the first holder of the title Bishop of Razès created in 1226). His successor was Bertrand Marti, who died on the fire in Montségur on 16 March 1244.

Peyrepertuse Castle, also called the "heavenly Carcassonne".

Quéribus Castle, one of the emblematic sites of the Cathar tragedy.

Raymond of Péreille and Pierre-Roger of Mirepoix (joint lords of Montségur)

The Péreille family came from the nobility of the region of Olmes. Its lands came under two feudal bodies: the Count of Foix and the Viscount of Béziers and Carcassonne. This fact helps us to understand one of the aspects of the complexity of the feudal system. In effect, two suzerains had rights over the Péreille family, which were obligations of service (military, legal) and also probably debts in kind and in cash, all falling under the eminent domain as opposed to the actual domain, namely the revenue from farming the land belonging to the Péreille family. It should be noted that, in turn, the two suzerains were the vassals of the Count of Toulouse (who, therefore, also owned the eminent domain).

Thus, Montségur really belonged to the Count of Toulouse, something which had a direct consequence when the Treaty of Paris was signed. The entire Olmes region was transferred from the dispossessed Count of Toulouse to Guy of Lévis, the direct vassal of the King of France, however, the two joint lords did not take account of this fact since, already in 1209, Simon de Montfort had given the castle to the same Guy of Lévis.

Raymond de Péreille was born around 1186 and married before 1222, but almost nothing is known about him until in around 1244. The other joint lord was his first cousin, Pierre-Roger de Mirepoix (heir to the rights of Montségur through his mother). The two cousins were almost the same age and in around 1239, Pierre-Roger married Raymond's daughter, Philippa, aged about 15 years (she was born in around 1225). Philippa was able to leave Montségur after the capitulation, but her mother and sister perished by fire.

Pierre-Roger de Mirepoix played a decisive role in the massacre in Avignonet because he supplied the executors (soldiers from Montségur) and organised the attack. He is said to have asked the executors for the skull of the Inquisitor Guillaume-Arnaud to use as a cup (but this had been destroyed by the many axe blows it had received).

Peyrepertuse Castle.

Article 16 of the Treaty of Paris makes a direct allusion to Montségur Castle and to its situation from a feudal point of view: "He (the King of France) left us (the Count of Toulouse) the entire diocese of Toulouse, except for the Terre du Maréchal (requested by us) which will belong to him (the King)". Therefore, Marshal Guy of Lévis received his fief from the King of France, something, which, in advance, provided a legal justification for the military action to capture the two lords occupying the domain as usurpers.

Naturally, the religious activity at Montségur had not escaped the attention of the Inquisition's officers and the representatives of French royal power: in particular, it was to Montségur that many Cathar believers travelled just before death to receive the consolamentum.

In March 1241, Raymond VII, on a visit to Saint Louis in Montargis (up until the end of the 17th century, with the construction of Versailles, the court of the King of France was itinerant) to take an oath (yet another) in which he recalled again that he was committed to "fighting in good faith the enemies of the King in the Albigensian region" and to destroying Montségur Castle "so that we can be its master" (an expression very much in the Count's style). Was there really a siege of Montségur following this oath? Specialists are far from being certain about this, in which case, it may have been yet another example of the Count of Toulouse's ambiguous attitude. In all cases, Montségur was not taken.

In 1242, the castle was still a focus of interest. One event in particular, which recalls the one in 1208 in Saint-Gilles, was going to lead directly to the loss of Montségur. Every visit by an Inquisition court stirred discontent in the regions and always involved a large number of people because the two Inquisitors were accompanied by representatives from the local clergy, from royal power and two auxiliaries (clerks, executioners no doubt, etc.). In 1241 and 1242, Inquisitors from Toulouse (the Dominican Guillaume-Arnaud and the Franciscan Etienne of Saint-Thiberi) set out to conduct a large series of inquiries in the south of the Albigensian region and in Lauragais.

On 28 May 1242, they spent the night in Avignonet, northwest of Castelnaudary, where the entire group (eleven people) was massacred, hacked to death by about fifty men mainly from Montségur, whose leaders were Faidit knights from the same castle. The operation was not fortuitous but had been prepared carefully.

Faidits

In the Middle Ages, this word referred to people on the run, people who had been banished, and, especially during the Albigensian crusade, Cathar heresy suspects, whose property had been confiscated, driven from their homes by the crusaders. Above all, the word applies to nobles dispossessed of their fiefs. Also, at the end of the 12th and the start of the 13th century, the verse of Gauveelm Faidit, a juggler-troubadour from Uzerche, who died in around 1220, was greatly appreciated by the Count of Toulouse.

An excommunication (another) was launched against Raymond VII, who was seen as being directly responsible for this collective massacre. In the previous months, Raymond VII had been preparing a new insurrection against the French royal forces and allies and this was launched at about the same time as the Avignonet affair. The Count of Toulouse's reconquest of his territory was very quick (July-August), with an attack from the Bordeaux region by Henry II of England, whose support had been obtained by Raymond to fight the King of France.

Quéribus Castle.

When trying to analyse the course of events and understand the facts, it is difficult not to notice the divide which existed between the ambitions (often small and petty) of these feudal lords who changed sides almost as often as they took an oath of fealty, and the human drama resulting from the movement of troops and the fighting. Behind the incessant about-faces, the final destruction of the Cathar heresy was already beginning to emerge.

At the end of August 1242, the Anglo-Occitan coalition collapsed. Raymond VII travelled to Lorris (in Gâtinais, therefore within royal French land, far from Toulouse) in January 1243 to meet Saint Louis and, again, to obtain an oath of loyalty from his vassals to the King and to the Christian faith, something which was obtained in February and March.

The siege of Montségur Castle

The lords of Montségur (the de facto ones because the rightful lord, Guy of Lévis, did not occupy the castle) had not taken the oath. Their fate was discussed at a council held in Béziers in April 1243 (note that Raymond VII asked this council to withdraw the excommunication against him after the assassination of Avignonet almost a year earlier). It was the royal seneschal of Carcassonne, Hugues of Arcis, who took command of military operations against Montségur, with the help of French and local troops taking advantage of the knights' period of ost. He was helped by the fact that, once again, forays were considered to be a crusade and were preached as such. The religious control of this foray was the responsibility of the Archbishop of Narbonne, Pierre Amiel.

The siege started at the end of May 1243. After much detailed research, Michel Roquebert believes there to have been about 360 people in the castle at that time, including 211 Perfects and just over a hundred fighters. But, little is known about the "civilian" refugees, namely the women, children and simple believers. The siege was exceptionally long lasting nine months. This may be explained by the attackers' inability to seal the area and, above all, to demolish the walls with catapults because of the site's topography.

Quéribus Castle.

The attackers had two problems to overcome. Firstly, to completely surround the site, which was difficult both because of the lie of the land and also because, naturally, the besieged knew the area much better than they did. It is more than likely that Montségur, through the emblematic role it had played over the past three decades, not only benefited from the friendship of the neighbouring population, but also from real support from outside the region. It is not certain whether, despite their numbers (believed to be ten thousand), the French royal forces and their local allies, there under duress or voluntarily, actually succeeded in completely surrounding the castle. However, one fact does support this theory, namely the arrival of reinforcements and technicians at the castle.

The second problem was victory itself. It was necessary to wait until October for any noticeable breakthroughs when Basque mountain dwellers managed to climb and set foot on the narrow platform on the eastern side of the plateau. This was 80 metres below the castle and was the only possible access route because the western part was defended by fortifications. The Cathars were unable to oust the attackers on the conquered platform.

In November, the royal forces experienced another success. The Bishop of Albi, who had arrived with reinforcements, may also have been an engineer and he had a catapult made which he installed on the conquered platform.

However, the occupants of the besieged castle fought back and a Cathar engineer managed to make his way through the attackers to the castle and built a war machine which was used to bombard the area conquered by the royal forces (middle December).

At the end of December, around Christmas time, there was a decisive event. The attackers managed to take the eastern tower by surprise, and even today, it is still uncertain which route they used. It was at this moment that those in charge of the castle had a treasure (gold and silver) secretly removed with the help of the troops laying siege to the castle. It is easy to imagine the dreams, fantasies and searches generated by the thought of this treasure!

The engineer who had been there in the middle of December returned (which proves that there was a certain amount of to-ing and fro-ing) to build a new machine (end of January).

A counter attack at the end of February 1244 to win back the eastern tower failed and taking advantage of the retreat, the royal forces attempted to enter the castle, but were driven back. It was the end! The two lords requested negotiations and accepted the conditions of surrender: fifteen days to hand over the site, the pardon of all acts including the massacre of Avignonet, a small penitence for the men of arms (fighters) and those who abjured, and death by fire for those who refused to abjure.

During the fifteen day truce, three or four Perfects managed to escape with the accord of Pierre-Roger of Mirepoix. Cathar believers decided to take the consolamentum.

When the time came between 210 and 215 people refused to abjure: probably 190 Perfects and about twenty believers. They were sentenced to death by fire, probably at the site's south-western facade. They were enclosed inside a wooden fence and a fire was lit under the dried wood and resin. The victims were not tied to stakes or strangled and died burnt alive (16 March 1244).

After Montségur

The fall of Montségur and the death by fire of the Perfects did not put an end to Catharism. Some refuges and centres still existed, such as Quéribus Castle (taken in 1255), but the victory was very much that of the Catholic Church (at what price!). The Inquisition continued to extend its empire despite resistance from French royal power and, in 1291, King Philip the Fair intervened to forbid royal officers from obeying the Inquisitors.

In political terms, the mechanisms introduced by the treaty were working. In 1249, a few months after burning a group of 80 heretics, whose trial had been so brief that even the procedures of the Inquisition had not been followed, the Count of Toulouse Raymond VII died without leaving a legitimate son. Once again, the question needs to be asked about the true personality of this man. Why such an act at such a time? To win the favour of the Church? Why all these oaths and about-faces followed by new oaths?

Aerial view of Quéribus Castle.

The new rulers of the county were Alfonso of Poitiers, Louis IX's brother, and his wife Joan, the only daughter of Raymond VII. Alfonso only travelled to Toulouse twice: in 1251 to receive the oath from his vassals, and in 1270. As a good administrator of French policy he reorganised the local tax system.

The couple died in 1271 and the county became a province of France.

Some names stand out from the dark years of the end of Catharism, for example, that of Pierre Authié, notary of the county of Foix. He left for Italy in around 1296 in order to follow teaching to become a Perfect. The campaign against the Cathars forced the practice of the Cathar faith underground and prevented the functioning of training centres but the Cathar Church still had centres of support in Italy. Pierre Authié and his brother Guilhem returned to the county of Foix in around 1299 and started their preaching work under imaginably difficult conditions. Pierre was arrested in 1309, tried and sentenced to death by fire. The sentence was carried out on 10 April 1310.

The last known case was that of Guilhem Bélibaste, born in around 1280 and sentenced to death by fire in 1321 outside Villerouge-Termenès Castle, where, in 1305, he had killed a shepherd who was an informant close to the Inquisition. After becoming a Perfect, he worked as a tradesman in the province of Teruel, but after marrying, he lost his title for having violated the obligation of chastity. When he was arrested, he refused to abjure his faith and was burned alive, as was his wife in 1325 in Carcassonne. The Italian Cathar Church, which had sent a message of support to the occupants under siege at Montségur, disappeared after 1412. The very last official Cathar church was in Bosnia and disappeared with the Ottoman invasion in 1463.

In the footsteps of the Cathars

Suggestions for a Cathar itinerary

A visit to the region of the Cathars should not be limited to visiting the Cathar "castles". Although the passage of time has left very few remains, some places still carry too many memories for them to be ignored. Instead of opting for a "signposted" itinerary, in what follows we will offer a few suggestions to help visitors to discover architectural reminders of this great Cathar tragedy.

Visitors must remember that the events took place over an area corresponding to about ten of our present-day departments.

Aude was the heart of the Cathar region. It was here that most of the Cathar "castles" were to be found: from east to west Aguilar, Quéribus, Villerouge-Termenès, Peyrepertuse, Termes, Puilaurens, Puivert and, further north the four castles of Lastours. Do not forget Alet (a Cathar lord had a Cathar abbot appointed here by force) and Pieusse (Cathar council in 1226), as well as Fontfroide Abbey (southwest of Narbonne), Fanjeaux with its evocation of the Dominicans and, above all, Bram, the town of martyrs, the same as Les Cassés.

In Ariège, the site of Montségur draws many visitors, but Montaillou, Mirepoix, Pamiers and Foix are also worth a visit.

In Tarn-et-Garonne, Moissac, with its famous capitals, was a site of many massacres and deaths by fire (210 heretics were burnt there in 1234) and Montauban was a pillar in the defence of Toulouse.

Cordes-sur-Ciel in Tarn is maybe the town the most reminiscent of its Cathar past. The term Albigensian crusade owes much to the exemplary nature of the repression of Cathar heretics in the town of Albi (it was there that the bodies of Cathars were exhumed and burned). Rabastens was also a centre of the Cathar faith and Lavaur was known for the large-scale death by fire organised there (between 300 and 400 people).

At the risk of lengthening the journey, do not forget Avignonet (Haute-Garonne), Toulouse of course (outside which Simon de Montfort perished), and Muret (where the King of Aragon was killed).

If the visitor studies a little local history, he will find many other reminders of the Cathars in southern Occitania.

View of Quéribus, north side.
Photo J. Debru.

The ruins of Cabaret in Lastours Castle.

Minerve Castle in Hérault, northwest of Narbonne.

The Cathar "castles"

This expression is commonly used in reference to the castles where the events of the war or the massacres of the Albigensian crusade took place. But it would be wrong to assimilate the present-day aspect of these fortresses, very often in ruins, to what they would have resembled at the time of the Cathars. The tribulations of history (systematic destruction after sieges, reconstruction when the region became French and the area formed the border region with Spain, and the abandonment of this line of fortifications), make these ruins very evocative of a dramatic past rather than the expression of a historic event.

Minerve Castle

This castle is in the south of Hérault, on the border with Aude. It owes its unfortunate reputation to the fact that it was the site of the very first death by fire of Cathars in the crusade. Simon de Montfort was urged to conquer it by some inhabitants of Narbonne, who saw it as a means to rid themselves of their wine-making competitors (personal interest was often a major aspect of operations).

The village, situated on a rocky outcrop lined by two gullies, was shared with the castle which closed the access to the plateau. Very little of this building remains.

Termes Castle

The castle, of which there are still some remains, in particular a window (much photographed!) in the shape of a cross, stood at the summit of a 470-metre high peak. It was accessible mainly from the south, with the north side opening out on to an 80-metre high sheer cliff, the east side on to very steep slopes, the same as the west side, although slightly less steep. The siege lasted four months, from August to November 1210, after the taking of Minerve. Raymond, the lord of Termes, was from the same family as Guillaume of Minerve.

The lord's family of Termes was actively involved in the Cathar faith. Raymond's brother took part, on the Cathar side, in the controversy with the Catholic prelates in Montréal (1207). He became the Bishop (Cathar) of Razès and was a participant at the Council (Cathar) in Pieusse in 1226.

During the siege, the crusader's army used several war machines, one of which was the work of the engineering skills of an archdeacon from Paris, Guillaume, who took part in the crusade. These machines enabled Simon de Montfort to damage and then take a tower ("termenet") on the frontline of the fortifications protecting the south side of the castle.

It was the lack of water and, above all the pollution of the water tanks, which forced Raymond of Termes to capitulate. In actual fact, the garrison abandoned the castle surreptitiously. Raymond was arrested when he returned to the castle and died in prison in Carcassonne in 1213.

Simon de Montfort gave the castle to a crusader, Alain of Roucy. Raymond's sons, who became faidits, fought among the Cathar ranks until 1227, with one of them, Olivier, remaining until 1240. He joined Louis IX on his journey to the Holy Land, took part in the Battle of Baltim (where the King of France was taken prisoner), spent one year in Cyprus on his way home and was present at the siege of Quéribus Castle, the last Cathar site defeated in 1255, but this time on the side of the royal forces. He returned to the Holy Land in 1264, then from 1267 to 1270, and then one more time for a final period. He died in 1275.

Alain of Roucy, the new owner of the seigniory took part in the Battle of Muret (1213) and, in particular, played a part in the death of Peter II of Aragon. He was awarded new seigniories for his work: Bram, famous for the torture of its inhabitants, and Montréal. He died in Montréal in 1228, besieged by the Counts of Toulouse and Foix during their revolt after the defeat and death of Simon de Montfort outside Toulouse.

In 1224, the castle was transferred to the Archbishop of Narbonne before being transferred to the King of France in 1228. The King turned it into a border fortress and established a royal garrison there. It was demolished in 1653 on a decision of Louis XIV who considered it to be superfluous and too expensive to maintain. After many changes, in 1915, the ruins became the property of the Touring Club of France until 1988. It is now the property of the commune.

Left:
Termes Castle.
Situated on a 470-metre peak, access was very difficult.
Photo J. Debru.

A cross-shaped loophole in the chapel of Termes Castle.
Photo J. Debru.

Puivert Castle.
Before becoming part of the Cathar tragedy, this castle was a renowned cultural centre famous for its poetry contests.

Right:
The interior courtyard of Puivert Castle.

Puivert Castle

Before being laid siege to and taken by Simon de Montfort in November 1210 (after Minerve and Termes), Puivert Castle was relatively famous at the end of the 12th century because it provided the venue for the poetry contest in which the major troubadours participated. Eleanor of Aquitaine, Louis VII's wife, and Henry II of England spent time there.

The seigniory held by Bernard of Congost supported the Cathar cause. Sicard of Puivert took part in the massacre of the Inquisitors at Avignonet (1242) and defended Montségur, and Saissa of Congost, a Perfect, perished in the fire of Montségur (1244).

The siege only lasted three days, with the Cathar defenders succeeding in escaping. The castle was given either to Pons of Brugères or to Lambert of Thury (documents are contradictory).

The site's topography has changed since Cathar times. A lake used to be situated below the castle and disappeared in 1279, swallowed up by the earth. A new artificial lake was created in recent years. Most of the ruins visible today date from the 13th and 14th centuries.

Montségur Castle

This castle owes its fame to the fact that it was the site where, on 16 March 1244,

Montségur Castle.

on the orders of the Inquisition and the royal power, more than two hundred Perfects were executed by fire. The site is a limestone plateau or "pog" surrounded by 80 to 150-metre high cliffs and covers about 5 hectares (700 metres long by 60 to 150 metres wide). The castle itself was built at an altitude of more than 1,200 metres at the centre of what was the "Cathar region" in the Ariège Pyrenees.

Nothing is known about the castle prior to the reconstruction undertaken in 1204 on request of the Cathar ecclesiastical authorities. The exact word used to describe this new fortified complex was "castrum", meaning a keep, a corps de logis (castellum) and a village, all surrounded by a wall. Excavation work in around 1947, and, in particular, more archaeological based work carried out from 1964 onwards, still does not give a very complete idea of what this castrum was.

Schematically, on the plateau, from east to west, it is possible to distinguish, the tower rock, a tower, a ditch, and the actual castle said to be defended on the west by a wall and specific fortifications.

At the end of the 13th century, the castle, which was one of the defensive features of the French border, was rebuilt and it is these ruins which are visible today.

Peyrepertuse Castle

This was the largest Cathar castle, also known as the "heavenly Carcassonne".

In the framework of the feudal system, the seigniory of Peyrepertuse was part of the Viscountcy of Narbonne and of the Kingdom of Aragon. It does not appear to have been affected by the crusaders' military action. In 1217, Guilhem of Peyrepertuse paid homage to Simon de Montfort clarifying that he was the vassal of Aymar, Viscount of Narbonne. In 1219, he took part in the revolt against the crusaders and occupied Puilaurens Castle. He was excommunicated. Proof of the complexity of feudal ties, the other suzerain, the King of Aragon (in this case the regent because the heir to King Peter II, who died in Muret, was a minor) had paid homage to the King of France in 1226 and sold the castle to Louis IX.

France only took possession of Peyrepertuse in 1240 after a three-day siege. As was the case with many other strongholds in the region, it became one of the links in the chain defending the border with Spain. Its position was ideal, situated on an 800-metre high crest with access via the northern facade. The church, the tower-tank and the dwelling in the old keep date from the start of the 12th century with the fortifications dating from the middle of the 13th century.

Aerial view of Peyrepertuse Castle.
Photo R. Cast.

Aguilar Castle.
Although built in a strategic location, this castle remained apart from the crusade against the Cathars.

Puilaurens Castle (formerly "Puylaurens")

This was the southernmost castle in the Kingdom of France. Its situation in the feudal system was similar to that of Peyrepertuse, the fate of which it also followed.

It was built on a semi-circular rocky outcrop at an altitude of 697 metres and has preserved many features from the Cathar period.

Quéribus Castle

This castle is situated on one of the crests on the southern border of the Corbières hills. After belonging to both the County of Besalu and the Viscountcy of Narbonne, the seigniory of Quéribus became part of the Kingdom of Aragon in 1162 and formed one of the elements of its northern border. The Viscountcy of Narbonne still owned the actual domain, namely the revenue from the land.

The castle remained apart from the armed fighting during the crusade but it did provide a refuge.

In 1239, the regent of the Kingdom of Aragon sold it along with Peyrepertuse Castle to Louis IX. However, this did not prevent Quéribus from continuing to be a centre of the Cathar faith, which explains the attacks on it in 1255 led by Pierre d'Auteuil, the seneschal (French) of Carcassonne with the help of the Archbishop of Narbonne. The castle capitulated under conditions which remain unclear.

Today, all that remains of the 12th century construction are the southern foundation of the keep and the external defensive structure on the keep's eastern side.

Aguilar Castle

Astonishingly in view of its strategic location (it was the easternmost link in the chain of Cathar castles, near Narbonne). Aguilar was not affected by the forays. At that time, it belonged to the Termes family, vassals of Trencavel, the Viscount of Béziers and Carcassonne. No events in the war took place there. Olivier of Termes, after taking part in the final revolt in 1240, surrendered to Louis IX after already having done so in 1228.

After becoming part of the Kingdom of France, the castle became an element in the border's line of defence until the signature of the Treaty of the Pyrenees.

Left page, top:
Puilaurens Castle, which has kept many features from the 13th century.

Bottom:
Quéribus Castle.
Situated on one of the peaks of the Hautes Corbières (north of Perpignan), this castle was one of the last Cathar refuges. It "fell" in 1255.
Photo R. Cast.

Lastours Castle.
This castle is in fact several castles.
It is actually formed by four strongholds stretching from north to south: Quertinheux, Surdespine, Régine Tower and Cabaret.

Lastours Castles

It is necessary to use the plural here because, in actual fact, there were four strongholds stretching from south to north, Quertinheux, Surdespine, Tour Régine and Cabaret. It is the latter whose name appears frequently in the chronicles of the fight against the Cathars and, in actual fact, refers to all four elements.

The complex is situated on a rocky outcrop about 600 metres long surrounded by two very deep valleys. The region, which takes the name of Cabardès, supported the Viscount of Béziers and Carcassonne. At the end of the 12th century, it turned to the Cathar faith and, during forays, the strongholds were used as a refuge for Perfects and believers and a centre for guerrilla activities. The presence of practising Perfects in Cabaret is testified to in around 1280, namely well after the castles of Montségur and Quéribus were taken by the royal forces, showing that these two events had not wiped out the Cathar heresy.

In fact, what is original about these four strongholds, and above all Cabaret, is the fact that they were never the subject of a long siege, massacre or death by fire. However, there was much fighting very nearby. In 1209, the Duke of Burgundy failed to take Cabaret, and Bouchard of Marly (a companion of Simon de Montfort) was taken prisoner. The tortured inhabitants of Bram were sent there by the crusaders in 1210 (their eyes gouged out and noses cut off). In 1211, Pierre-Roger of Cabaret, one of the leaders of the Cathar resistance, agreed an exchange with the crusaders: the castle and its prisoner Bouchard of Marly in exchange for other domains. He recovered his fief a few years later, but after resisting Humbert of Beaujeu in 1227, he became the vassal of the King of France with the Treaty of Paris and the four strongholds becoming royal citadels.

Nothing remains of the castles built from about 1050 to about 1150. However, elements are visible which were built or rebuilt in around 1240.

Villerouge-Termenès Castle

It was outside this castle, in August 1321, that the last known Perfect, Guillaume Bélibaste, was burned alive. It was the property of the Archbishop of Narbonne at least from 1107 to the French Revolution. The main part of the building dates from the third quarter of the 13th century. The keep was built at the start of the 14th century.

Villerouge-Termenes Castle.
In 1210, this castle survived a siege of several months. It was here that the very last known "Perfect" was burned: Guillaume Bélibaste.

Chronology

> 1167
Cathar council in Saint-Félix Lauragais; creation of four Cathar bishops.

> 1177
Letter from Raymond V to the Order of Cîteaux informing him of the fearsome spread of the Cathar heresy.

> 1194-1222
Reign of Raymond VI, Count of Toulouse.

> 1198-1216
Pontificate of Innocent III.

> 1204
Controversy between Cathars and Catholics in Carcassonne under the initiative of the King of Aragon. Open conversion to the Cathar faith by the sister of the Count of Foix, Esclarmonde.

> 1206
Start of Dominican preaching.

> 1207
New controversy in Montréal.

> 1208
Assassination of the legate Pierre de Castelnau in Saint-Gilles.

> 1209
Start of the Albigensian crusade with the massacre of Béziers. Simon de Montfort becomes Viscount of Béziers and Carcassonne.

> 1210
Executions by fire in Minerve.

> 1211
Executions by fire in Lavaur and Les Cassès.

> 1213
False end to and resumption of the crusade. Battle of Muret, defeat of the Occitans supported by Aragon. Death of Peter II.

> 1214
Executions by fire in Morlhon.

> 1215
Simon de Montfort, Count of Toulouse. Council of the Lateran.

> 1218
Death of Simon de Montfort during the siege of Toulouse.

> 1219
Massacre of Marmande.

> 1222-1249
Reign of Raymond VII, Count of Toulouse.

> 1224
Amaury, Simon de Montfort's son, transfers his rights over the region to the King of France.

> 1226
Crusade in the Albigensian region by Louis VIII. Cathar Council of Pieusse with the appointment of a fifth bishop.

> 1229
Treaty of Paris.

> 1231
Creation of the Inquisition by Pope Gregory IX, who entrusted the Dominican Order with pursuing heretics and eradicating the heresy in Languedoc and Provence.

> 1242
Assassination of Inquisition collaborators in Avignonet.

> 1243-1244
Siege of Montségur and deaths by fire.

> 1249
Executions by fire in Agen. Alfonso of Poitiers, Saint Louis' brother, becomes Count of Toulouse.

> 1255
Capitulation of Quéribus.

> 1258
Treaty of Corbeil.

> 1271
Death of Alfonso of Poitiers and his wife. Incorporation of the County of Toulouse into the royal French domain.

Bibliography

Those wishing to develop their knowledge of the Cathars now have access to a serious and enjoyable collection of books, something which was not the case two or three decades ago because, for many years the wealth of titles often hid a lack of research.

For us, the main reference work is the series of four volumes by Michel Roquebert entitled L'Epopée Cathare (éditions Privat in Toulouse). The author has analysed the records drawn up by the Inquisitors, the content of which has helped us to learn a wealth of details about the personality and lives of heresy suspects.

Based on an identical working method, Jean Duvernoy has written (also by Privat) La Religion des Cathares et Histoire des Cathares, an equally serious work, unlike many other publications on Cathar religion, a subject in which fantasy and imagination are commonplace.

Special reference should be made to an already ancient publication by Achille Luchaire, La Croisade des Albigeois (published at the start of the century), a book which is very surprising for its time and is filled with the radical and centralising principles of the teachings of the 3rd Republic. In actual fact, this book by a leading medieval history specialist focuses on the destructive and invasive aspects of the French troops in Occitania. Such a regionalist tone is very astonishing for the period when this book was prepared and published. Of course, since then, the documentation base has been greatly enriched thanks to the analysis of the Inquisition's registers and, as a result, some of Luchaire's assessments need to be revised.

Nevertheless, if you want to allow your imagination to roam, you can always read or browse Histoire des Albigeois (in three volumes) by N. Peyrat published in 1880. Apart from the weaknesses, errors and exaggerations found in this work, tribute should be paid to the author who brought back to life an episode in Occitan history and Cathar religious life forgotten for many years after their disappearance.

Many more publications on general or specific aspects of the Cathar drama could be cited, but we have chosen intentionally to focus on the main ones in the strictest sense of the word. We could also mention the work by Anne Brenon, Les Cathares, Pauvres du Christ ou Apôtres de Satan, in the Découvertes Gallimard collection published in 1997, a small and well-illustrated book which, above all, deals with the religious aspects of the Cathar tragedy and which sets the record straight on certain divergences in interpretations and the historical reality of "Cathar castles".

LOT
Rodez
Aveyron
Bas Quercy
AVEYRON
Causse Méjean
TARN-ET-
Ségala
Moissac
Millau
Aveyron
Cordes
Montauban
GARONNE
Causse du Larzac
Albi
Tarn
Tarn
Garonne
TARN
Rabastens
Lombers
Lodévois
Graulhet
HÉRA
GERS
Lavaur
Save
Agout
Toulouse
Castres
LANGUEDOC-ROUSSILLON
MIDI-PYRÉNÉES
Lauragais
Hérault
Muret
St-Félix-Lauragais
Minervois
Canal du Midi
Montagne Noire
Minerve
Les Cassés
Avignonet
Béziers
Castelnaudary
Lastours
HAUTE-GARONNE
Aude
Bram
Carcassonne
Volvestre
Fanjeaux
Montréal
Narbonne
AUDE
Pamiers
Fontfroide
Mirepoix
Pieusse
Corbières
Limoux
Alet
Termes
Razès
Arques
Villerouge-Termenès
Foix
ARIÈGE
Puivert
Montségur
Peyrepertuse
Aguilar
Quillan
Couserans
Ariège
Montaillou
Puilaurens
Quéribus
Fenouillet
Perpignan
Têt
PYRÉNÉES-ORIENTALES
ESPAGNE
ANDORRE
50 km

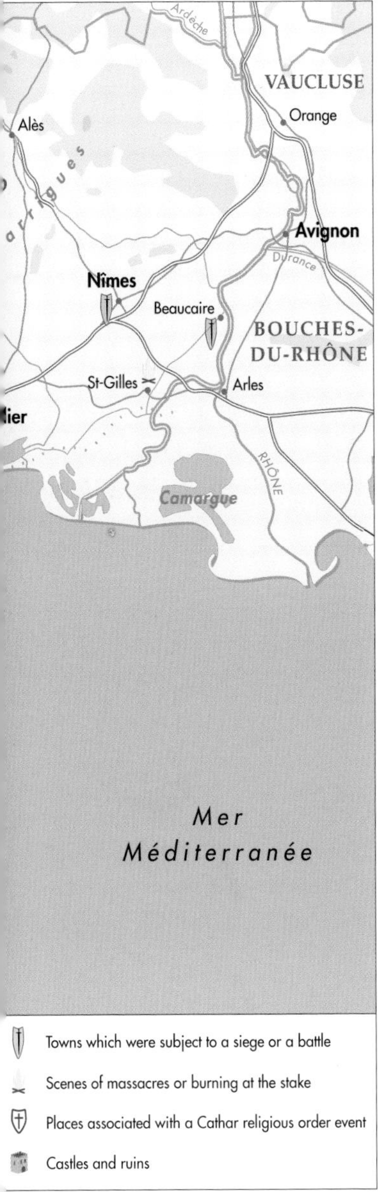

Index of place names

A

Agen *36, 48, 53, 67*
Aguilar *113, 119*
Albi *11, 18, 36, 48, 53, 58, 60, 68, 70, 82, 94, 99, 103, 113*
Aragon *25, 26, 27, 29, 31, 32, 33 64, 74, 77, 117, 119, 122*
Avignon *86, 93, 94*
Avignonet *106, 107, 108, 109, 110,113, 116, 122*

B

Beaucaire *58, 86, 94*
Béziers *26, 27, 53, 55, 58, 60, 61, 62, 64, 71, 73, 74, 82, 88, 89, 91, 94, 104, 109, 119, 120, 122*
Bourges *52, 90, 91, 92*
Bram *68, 69, 70, 113, 115, 120*

C

Castelnaudary *58, 70, 71, 94, 107*
Castres *53, 58, 66, 94*
Cavaillon *62*
Comminges *26, 53, 74*

F

Fanjeaux *68, 79, 113*
Foix *11, 26, 27, 36, 51, 81, 104, 111,113*

L

Lastours *113, 120*
Lavaur *53, 58, 67, 70, 78, 94, 113, 122*
Limoux *66, 92*
Lombers *48, 68*

M

Marmande *87, 88, 122*
Millau *27*
Minerve *70, 72, 88, 113, 116*
Montpellier *26, 27, 55, 60, 62, 72, 82, 83, 87, 99*
Montségur *13, 18, 47, 67, 95, 100, 104, 105, 106, 107, 109, 110, 111, 113, 116, 120, 123*
Montréal *55, 58, 69, 104, 115, 122*
Muret *35, 79, 80, 81, 113, 115, 117, 122*

N

Narbonne *26, 31, 52, 53, 62, 72, 81, 83, 88, 89, 102, 113, 114, 117, 119, 121*
Nîmes *87, 94*

P

Pamiers *58, 68, 76, 77, 94, 113*
Peyrepertuse *113, 117, 119*
Pont-de-l'Arche *85*
Puilaurens *94, 113, 117, 119*
Puivert *70, 113, 116*

Q-S

Quéribus *47, 11, 113, 115, 119, 120, 122*
Saint-Félix Lauragais *36, 48, 122*
Saint-Gilles *55, 56, 71, 72, 97, 107, 122*

T

Termes *70, 88, 113, 114, 116, 119*

Carcassonne and Toulouse are cited too often to appear in this index.

The ramparts of Carcassonne.

Index of peoples' names

In view of the fact that, at the time (13th century), family names and their spelling had not yet been defined, it is not surprising to see that these vary in the documents. In order to facilitate searches, this index is based on the first word (which often, later, was going to become the first name in the modern sense) of the person's overall name.

A
Alfonso of Poitiers, brother of Saint Louis *33*
Alfonso II, King of Aragon *31, 33*
Amaury of Montfort *86, 87, 88, 89, 97, 103, 122*
Arnaud-Amaury of Montfort, abbot of Cîteaux *54, 55, 56, 58, 60, 62, 64, 65, 72, 78, 81, 82, 83, 102*

B-C
Blanche of Castille, mother of Saint Louis *95, 97*
Chrétien de Troyes *10*

E
Eleanor of Aquitaine *52, 116*

F-G
Frederick II, Emperor *90, 93, 103, 104*
Guilhabert of Castres *105*
Guilhen Bélibaste *111*

H
Henry II, King of England *31, 116*
Honorius III, pope *89*
Humbert of Beaujeu *94, 95, 121*
Hugues of Arcis *109*

I-J
Innocent III, Pope *17, 19, 20, 22, 53, 54, 55, 57, 58, 62, 63, 78, 81, 83, 84, 90, 122*
John Lackland, King of England *22, 33, 81*

L
Louis VIII, King of France *32, 33, 57, 83, 89, 90, 92, 93, 94, 95, 98, 122*
Louis IX, King of France *33, 95, 97, 99, 104, 111, 115, 117, 119*

P
Philip II Augustus *22, 32, 33, 55, 56, 57, 58, 63, 83, 85, 88, 89, 90, 92*
Pierre Authié *111*
Peter II, King of Aragon *32, 33, 60, 64, 66, 68, 73, 77, 78, 79, 80, 115, 117, 122*
Pierre de Bénevent *81, 82*
Pierre de Castelnau, legate *53, 54, 55, 71, 72, 122*
Pierre-Roger of Mirepoix *105, 106, 110*

R
Raoul of Fontfroide *54*
Raymond VI, Count of Toulouse *32, 55, 56, 71, 73, 74, 77, 78, 79, 81, 82, 83, 85, 86, 87, 122*
Raymond VII, Count of Toulouse *11, 87, 90, 92, 93, 95, 96, 97, 98, 102, 103, 104, 107, 108, 109, 110, 111, 122*
Raymond of Péreille *104, 106*
Roger II Trencavel *53, 60, 64, 68, 87*

S
Saint Dominic *55, 100, 103*
Saint Louis, King of France: *see Louis IX*
Simon de Montfort *7, 11, 24, 57, 58, 62, 63, 64, 65, 66, 68, 69, 70, 71, 72, 73, 74, 75, 79, 80, 81, 82, 83, 84, 85, 86, 87, 88, 97, 103, 104, 106, 113, 114, 115, 116, 117, 120, 122*

The Pyrenees, seen from the Pic du Midi observatory.

Contents

6 Problems of vocabulary, diverging viewpoints

12 The context and the players
13 *The feudal regime*
18 *The Church*
25 *Political aspects*

34 The Cathar religion

46 The unfolding of events
47 *The situation at the start of the 13th century*
56 *The first crusade against the Cathars (1209-1213)*
81 *The completion of the conquest (1214-1215)*
86 *The revolt: successes and setbacks (1216-1225)*
92 *The "French solution" (1226-1229)*
100 *Montségur, the end of the Cathars (1244)*

112 In the footsteps of the Cathars
113 *Suggestions for a Cathar itinerary*
114 *The "Cathar" castles*

122 Appendices
122 *Chronology*
123 *Bibliography*
125 *Index of place names*
126 *Index of peoples' names*

Editor
Christian Ryo

Editorial coordination
Caroline Brou

Editorial collaboration
Maud Poupa and
Caroline Decaudin

Graphic design
Alexandre Chaize

Page layout
Studio graphique
des Éditions Ouest-France

Cartography
AFDEC

Photoengraving
Micro Lynx (35)

Printing
Gibert Clarey Imprimeurs
in Chambray-lès-Tours (37)

Édilarge S.A., Rennes
ISBN 978-2-7373-6276-7
Legal deposit: January 2015
Publisher's No.:
7380.01.0,5.01.15
printed in France

www.editionsouestfrance.fr